Taxation in an
Integrating World

Integrating National Economies: Promise and Pitfalls

Barry Bosworth (Brookings Institution) and Gur Ofer (Hebrew University)
Reforming Planned Economies in an Integrating World Economy

Ralph C. Bryant (Brookings Institution)
International Coordination of National Stabilization Policies

Susan M. Collins (Brookings Institution/Georgetown University)
Distributive Issues: A Constraint on Global Integration

Richard N. Cooper (Harvard University)
Environment and Resource Policies for the World Economy

Ronald G. Ehrenberg (Cornell University)
Labor Markets and Integrating National Economies

Barry Eichengreen (University of California, Berkeley)
International Monetary Arrangements for the 21st Century

Mitsuhiro Fukao (Bank of Japan)
Financial Integration, Corporate Governance, and the Performance of Multinational Companies

Stephan Haggard (University of California, San Diego)
Developing Nations and the Politics of Global Integration

Richard J. Herring (University of Pennsylvania) and Robert E. Litan (Department of Justice/Brookings Institution)
Financial Regulation in the Global Economy

Miles Kahler (University of California, San Diego)
International Institutions and the Political Economy of Integration

Anne O. Krueger (Stanford University)
Trade Policies and Developing Nations

Robert Z. Lawrence (Harvard University)
Regionalism, Multilateralism, and Deeper Integration

Sylvia Ostry (University of Toronto) and Richard R. Nelson (Columbia University)
Techno-Nationalism and Techno-Globalism: Conflict and Cooperation

Robert L. Paarlberg (Wellesley College/Harvard University)
Leadership Abroad Begins at Home: U.S. Foreign Economic Policy after the Cold War

Peter Rutland (Wesleyan University)
Russia, Eurasia, and the Global Economy

F. M. Scherer (Harvard University)
Competition Policies for an Integrated World Economy

Susan L. Shirk (University of California, San Diego)
How China Opened Its Door: The Political Success of the PRC's Foreign Trade and Investment Reforms

Alan O. Sykes (University of Chicago)
Product Standards for Internationally Integrated Goods Markets

Akihiko Tanaka (Institute of Oriental Culture, University of Tokyo)
The Politics of Deeper Integration: National Attitudes and Policies in Japan

Vito Tanzi (International Monetary Fund)
Taxation in an Integrating World

William Wallace (St. Antony's College, Oxford University)
Regional Integration: The West European Experience

Vito Tanzi

Taxation in an Integrating World

THE BROOKINGS INSTITUTION
Washington, D.C.

Library of Congress Cataloging-in-Publication data:
Taxation in an integrating world / Vito Tanzi.
p.   cm. — (Integrating national economies)
Includes bibliographical references and index.
ISBN 0-8157-8297-7—ISBN 0-8157-8298-5 (pbk.)
1. Taxation.   2. Income tax—Foreign income.   3. Capital levy.
4. International economic integration.   I. Series.
HJ2305.T187   1994
336.2—dc20   94-27337
                                                             CIP

9 8 7 6 5 4 3 2 1

The paper used in this publication meets the minimum requirements of
American National Standard for Information Sciences—Permanence of Paper
for Printed Library Materials, ANSI Z39.48-1984

Typeset in Plantin

Composition by Princeton Editorial Associates
Princeton, New Jersey

Printed by R. R. Donnelley and Sons Co.
Harrisonburg, Virginia

Foreword

MODERN tax systems were developed when countries' economies were relatively closed. At that time most of the incomes received by individuals or enterprises were domestic, and individuals and enterprises operated largely within one jurisdiction. Political and economic frontiers coincided fairly closely. The principles that came to guide tax relationships reflected these conditions.

The increasing globalization of economic activities and the growing integration of the world's economies have changed the economic environment, creating conflict between traditional principles and policies and current developments. Individuals and companies operating internationally pay income abroad and receive income from abroad. Capital and, to some extent, highly skilled labor have become more sensitive to differences in effective tax rates and react to these differences.

The implications of these changes for tax systems are enormous, and not fully understood. In this book Vito Tanzi, who is director of the Fiscal Affairs Department of the International Monetary Fund, attempts to address some of the key questions that arise in this changing environment. Drawing from his direct experience, he pays special attention to administrative and practical considerations that may limit the solutions that on purely theoretical grounds may appear optimal or, at least, desirable.

In writing this book the author received help from many individuals. He is particularly grateful to Henry Aaron for his comments, criticism, and encouragement, and to Joel Slemrod for thoughtful and useful comments on an early draft of this paper. Useful comments and assistance were also received from Ralph C. Bryant, Susan M. Collins, Edward H. Gardner, Hiromitsu Ishi, Robert Z. Lawrence, David Nellor, Anthony Pellechio, Victoria Summers, Emil Sunley, Alan Tait, and the participants at the Brookings seminar where the first draft of this book was presented. Anthony Pellechio provided assistance in the preparation of the appendix to chapter 7. Yvonne Liem, head of the IMF Fiscal Library, and Young-ja Kim were invaluable in tracing publications and assisting the author in many other ways. Champa Nguyen typed the manuscript, David Rossetti prepared it for editing and verification, Princeton Editorial Associates edited it and prepared the index, and David Bearce verified its factual content. Marc Rysman prepared the reference list.

Funding for the project came from the Center for Global Partnership of the Japan Foundation, the Curry Foundation, the Ford Foundation, the Korea Foundation, the Tokyo Club Foundation for Global Studies, the United States-Japan Foundation, and the Alex C. Walker Educational and Charitable Foundation. The author and Brookings are grateful for their support.

The views expressed in this book are those of the author and should not be ascribed to the persons or organizations whose assistance is acknowledged, to the International Monetary Fund, or to the trustees, officers, or staff members of the Brookings Institution.

BRUCE K. MACLAURY
President

November 1994
Washington, D.C.

Contents

Tables

Figures

Preface to the Studies on Integrating National Economies

ECONOMIC interdependence among nations has increased sharply in the past half century. For example, while the value of total production of industrial countries increased at a rate of about 9 percent a year on average between 1964 and 1992, the value of the exports of those nations grew at an average rate of 12 percent, and lending and borrowing across national borders through banks surged upward even more rapidly at 23 percent a year. This international economic interdependence has contributed to significantly improved standards of living for most countries. Continuing international economic integration holds out the promise of further benefits. Yet the increasing sensitivity of national economies to events and policies originating abroad creates dilemmas and pitfalls if national policies and international cooperation are poorly managed.

The Brookings Project on Integrating National Economies, of which this study is a component, focuses on the interplay between two fundamental facts about the world at the end of the twentieth century. First, the world will continue for the foreseeable future to be organized politically into nation-states with sovereign governments. Second, increasing economic integration among nations will continue to erode differences among national economies and undermine the autonomy of national governments. The project explores the opportunities and tensions arising from these two facts.

Scholars from a variety of disciplines have produced twenty-one studies for the first phase of the project. Each study examines the heightened competition between national political sovereignty and increased cross-border economic integration. This preface identifies background themes and issues common to all the studies and provides a brief overview of the project as a whole.[1]

Increasing World Economic Integration

Two underlying sets of causes have led nations to become more closely intertwined. First, technological, social, and cultural changes have sharply reduced the effective economic distances among nations. Second, many of the government policies that traditionally inhibited cross-border transactions have been relaxed or even dismantled.

The same improvements in transportation and communications technology that make it much easier and cheaper for companies in New York to ship goods to California, for residents of Strasbourg to visit relatives in Marseilles, and for investors in Hokkaido to buy and sell shares on the Tokyo Stock Exchange facilitate trade, migration, and capital movements spanning nations and continents. The sharply reduced costs of moving goods, money, people, and information underlie the profound economic truth that technology has made the world markedly smaller.

New communications technology has been especially significant for financial activity. Computers, switching devices, and telecommunications satellites have slashed the cost of transmitting information internationally, of confirming transactions, and of paying for transactions. In the 1950s, for example, foreign exchange could be bought and sold only during conventional business hours in the initiating party's time zone. Such transactions can now be carried out instantaneously twenty-four hours a day. Large banks pass the management of their worldwide foreign-exchange positions around the globe from one branch to another, staying continuously ahead of the setting sun.

Such technological innovations have increased the knowledge of potentially profitable international exchanges and of economic opportunities abroad. Those developments, in turn, have changed consumers' and producers' tastes. Foreign goods, foreign vacations, foreign financial investments—virtually anything from other nations—have lost some of their exotic character.

1. A complete list of authors and study titles is included at the beginning of this volume, facing the title page.

Although technological change permits increased contact among nations, it would not have produced such dramatic effects if it had been countermanded by government policies. Governments have traditionally taxed goods moving in international trade, directly restricted imports and subsidized exports, and tried to limit international capital movements. Those policies erected "separation fences" at the borders of nations. From the perspective of private sector agents, separation fences imposed extra costs on cross-border transactions. They reduced trade and, in some cases, eliminated it. During the 1930s governments used such policies with particular zeal, a practice now believed to have deepened and lengthened the Great Depression.

After World War II, most national governments began—sometimes unilaterally, more often collaboratively—to lower their separation fences, to make them more permeable, or sometimes even to tear down parts of them. The multilateral negotiations under the auspices of the General Agreement on Trade and Tariffs (GATT)—for example, the Kennedy Round in the 1960s, the Tokyo Round in the 1970s, and most recently the protracted negotiations of the Uruguay Round, formally signed only in April 1994—stand out as the most prominent examples of fence lowering for trade in goods. Though contentious and marked by many compromises, the GATT negotiations are responsible for sharp reductions in at-the-border restrictions on trade in goods and services. After the mid-1980s a large number of developing countries moved unilaterally to reduce border barriers and to pursue outwardly oriented policies.

The lowering of fences for financial transactions began later and was less dramatic. Nonetheless, by the 1990s government restrictions on capital flows, especially among the industrial countries, were much less important and widespread than at the end of World War II and in the 1950s.

By shrinking the economic distances among nations, changes in technology would have progressively integrated the world economy even in the absence of reductions in governments' separation fences. Reductions in separation fences would have enhanced interdependence even without the technological innovations. Together, these two sets of evolutionary changes have reinforced each other and strikingly transformed the world economy.

Changes in the Government of Nations

Simultaneously with the transformation of the global economy, major changes have occurred in the world's political structure. First, the number of governmental decisionmaking units in the world has expanded markedly and political power has been diffused more broadly among them. Rising nationalism and, in some areas, heightened ethnic tensions have accompanied that increasing political pluralism.

The history of membership in international organizations documents the sharp growth in the number of independent states. For example, only 44 nations participated in the Bretton Woods conference of July 1944, which gave birth to the International Monetary Fund. But by the end of 1970, the IMF had 118 member nations. The number of members grew to 150 by the mid-1980s and to 178 by December 1993. Much of this growth reflects the collapse of colonial empires. Although many nations today are small and carry little individual weight in the global economy, their combined influence is considerable and their interests cannot be ignored as easily as they were in the past.

A second political trend, less visible but equally important, has been the gradual loss of the political and economic hegemony of the United States. Immediately after World War II, the United States by itself accounted for more than one-third of world production. By the early 1990s the U.S. share had fallen to about one-fifth. Concurrently, the political and economic influence of the European colonial powers continued to wane, and the economic significance of nations outside Europe and North America, such as Japan, Korea, Indonesia, China, Brazil, and Mexico, increased. A world in which economic power and influence are widely diffused has displaced a world in which one or a few nations effectively dominated international decisionmaking.

Turmoil and the prospect of fundamental change in the formerly centrally planned economies compose a third factor causing radical changes in world politics. During the era of central planning, governments in those nations tried to limit external influences on their economies. Now leaders in the formerly planned economies are trying to adopt reforms modeled on Western capitalist principles. To the extent that these efforts succeed, those nations will increase their economic involvement with the rest of the world. Political and economic alignments among the Western industrialized nations will be forced to adapt.

Governments and scholars have begun to assess these three trends, but their far-reaching ramifications will not be clear for decades.

Dilemmas for National Policies

Cross-border economic integration and national political sovereignty have increasingly come into conflict, leading to a growing mismatch between the economic and political structures of the world. The effective domains of economic markets have come to coincide less and less with national governmental jurisdictions.

When the separation fences at nations' borders were high, governments and citizens could sharply distinguish "international" from "domestic" policies. International policies dealt with at-the-border barriers, such as tariffs and quotas, or responded to events occurring abroad. In contrast, domestic policies were concerned with everything behind the nation's borders, such as competition and antitrust rules, corporate governance, product standards, worker safety, regulation and supervision of financial institutions, environmental protection, tax codes, and the government's budget. Domestic policies were regarded as matters about which nations were sovereign, to be determined by the preferences of the nation's citizens and its political institutions, without regard for effects on other nations.

As separation fences have been lowered and technological innovations have shrunk economic distances, a multitude of formerly neglected differences among nations' domestic policies have become exposed to international scrutiny. National governments and international negotiations must thus increasingly deal with "deeper"—behind-the-border—integration. For example, if country A permits companies to emit air and water pollutants whereas country B does not, companies that use pollution-generating methods of production will find it cheaper to produce in country A. Companies in country B that compete internationally with companies in country A are likely to complain that foreign competitors enjoy unfair advantages and to press for international pollution standards.

Deeper integration requires analysis of the economic and the political aspects of virtually all nonborder policies and practices. Such

issues have already figured prominently in negotiations over the evo-
lution of the European Community, over the Uruguay Round of
GATT negotiations, over the North American Free Trade Agreement
(NAFTA), and over the bilateral economic relationships between
Japan and the United States. Future debates about behind-the-border
policies will occur with increasing frequency and prove at least as
complex and contentious as the past negotiations regarding at-the-
border restrictions.

Tensions about deeper integration arise from three broad sources:
cross-border spillovers, diminished national autonomy, and challenges
to political sovereignty.

Cross-Border Spillovers

Some activities in one nation produce consequences that spill
across borders and affect other nations. Illustrations of these spillovers abound. Given the impact of modern technology of banking
and securities markets in creating interconnected networks, lax rules
in one nation erode the ability of all other nations to enforce banking
and securities rules and to deal with fraudulent transactions. Given
the rapid diffusion of knowledge, science and technology policies in
one nation generate knowledge that other nations can use without full
payment. Labor market policies become matters of concern to other
nations because workers migrate in search of work; policies in one
nation can trigger migration that floods or starves labor markets
elsewhere. When one nation dumps pollutants into the air or water
that other nations breathe or drink, the matter goes beyond the
unitary concern of the polluting nation and becomes a matter for
international negotiation. Indeed, the hydrocarbons that are emitted
into the atmosphere when individual nations burn coal for generating
electricity contribute to global warming and are thereby a matter of
concern for the entire world.

The tensions associated with cross-border spillovers can be especially vexing when national policies generate outcomes alleged to be
competitively inequitable, as in the example in which country A
permits companies to emit pollutants and country B does not. Or
consider a situation in which country C requires commodities, whether
produced at home or abroad, to meet certain design standards, justified for safety reasons. Foreign competitors may find it too expensive

to meet these standards. In that event, the standards in C act very much like tariffs or quotas, effectively narrowing or even eliminating foreign competition for domestic producers. Citing examples of this sort, producers or governments in individual nations often complain that business is not conducted on a "level playing field." Typically, the complaining nation proposes that *other* nations adjust their policies to moderate or remove the competitive inequities.

Arguments for creating a level playing field are troublesome at best. International trade occurs precisely because of differences among nations—in resource endowments, labor skills, and consumer tastes. Nations specialize in producing goods and services in which they are relatively most efficient. In a fundamental sense, cross-border trade is valuable because the playing field is *not* level.

When David Ricardo first developed the theory of comparative advantage, he focused on differences among nations owing to climate or technology. But Ricardo could as easily have ascribed the productive differences to differing "social climates" as to physical or technological climates. Taking all "climatic" differences as given, the theory of comparative advantage argues that free trade among nations will maximize global welfare.

Taken to its logical extreme, the notion of leveling the playing field implies that nations should become homogeneous in all major respects. But that recommendation is unrealistic and even pernicious. Suppose country A decides that it is too poor to afford the costs of a clean environment, and will thus permit the production of goods that pollute local air and water supplies. Or suppose it concludes that it cannot afford stringent protections for worker safety. Country A will then argue that it is inappropriate for other nations to impute to country A the value they themselves place on a clean environment and safety standards (just as it would be inappropriate to impute the A valuations to the environment of other nations). The core of the idea of political sovereignty is to permit national residents to order their lives and property in accord with their own preferences.

Which perspective about differences among nations in behind-the-border policies is more compelling? Is country A merely exercising its national preferences and appropriately exploiting its comparative advantage in goods that are dirty or dangerous to produce? Or does a legitimate international problem exist that justifies pressure from other nations urging country A to accept changes in its policies (thus

curbing its national sovereignty)? When national governments negotiate resolutions to such questions—trying to agree whether individual
nations are legitimately exercising sovereign choices or, alternatively,
engaging in behavior that is unfair or damaging to other nations—the
dialogue is invariably contentious because the resolutions depend on
the typically complex circumstances of the international spillovers
and on the relative weights accorded to the interests of particular
individuals and particular nations.

Diminished National Autonomy

As cross-border economic integration increases, governments experience greater difficulties in trying to control events within their
borders. Those difficulties, summarized by the term *diminished autonomy*, are the second set of reasons why tensions arise from the competition between political sovereignty and economic integration.

For example, nations adjust monetary and fiscal policies to influence domestic inflation and employment. In setting these policies,
smaller countries have always been somewhat constrained by foreign
economic events and policies. Today, however, all nations are constrained, often severely. More than in the past, therefore, nations may
be better able to achieve their economic goals if they work together
collaboratively in adjusting their macroeconomic policies.

Diminished autonomy and cross-border spillovers can sometimes
be allowed to persist without explicit international cooperation to
deal with them. States in the United States adopt their own tax
systems and set policies for assistance to poor single people without
any formal cooperation or limitation. Market pressures operate to
force a degree of de facto cooperation. If one state taxes corporations
too heavily, it knows business will move elsewhere. (Those familiar
with older debates about "fiscal federalism" within the United States
and other nations will recognize the similarity between those issues
and the emerging international debates about deeper integration of
national economies.) Analogously, differences among nations in regulations, standards, policies, institutions, and even social and cultural
preferences create economic incentives for a kind of arbitrage that
erodes or eliminates the differences. Such pressures involve not only
the conventional arbitrage that exploits price differentials (buying at
one point in geographic space or time and selling at another) but also

shifts in the location of production facilities and in the residence of factors of production.

In many other cases, however, cross-border spillovers, arbitrage pressures, and diminished effectiveness of national policies can produce unwanted consequences. In cases involving what economists call externalities (external economies and diseconomies), national governments may need to cooperate to promote mutual interests. For example, population growth, continued urbanization, and the more intensive exploitation of natural resources generate external diseconomies not only within but across national boundaries. External economies generated when benefits spill across national jurisdictions probably also increase in importance (for instance, the gains from basic research and from control of communicable diseases).

None of these situations is new, but technological change and the reduction of tariffs and quotas heighten their importance. When one nation produces goods (such as scientific research) or "bads" (such as pollution) that significantly affect other nations, individual governments acting sequentially and noncooperatively cannot deal effectively with the resulting issues. In the absence of explicit cooperation and political leadership, too few collective goods and too many collective bads will be supplied.

Challenges to Political Sovereignty

The pressures from cross-border economic integration sometimes even lead individuals or governments to challenge the core assumptions of national political sovereignty. Such challenges are a third source of tensions about deeper integration.

The existing world system of nation-states assumes that a nation's residents are free to follow their own values and to select their own political arrangements without interference from others. Similarly, property rights are allocated by nation. (The so-called global commons, such as outer space and the deep seabed, are the sole exceptions.) A nation is assumed to have the sovereign right to exploit its property in accordance with its own preferences and policies. Political sovereignty is thus analogous to the concept of consumer sovereignty (the presumption that the individual consumer best knows his or her own interests and should exercise them freely).

In times of war, some nations have had sovereignty wrested from them by force. In earlier eras, a handful of individuals or groups have questioned the premises of political sovereignty. With the profound increases in economic integration in recent decades, however, a larger number of individuals and groups—and occasionally even their national governments—have identified circumstances in which, it is claimed, some universal or international set of values should take precedence over the preferences or policies of particular nations.

Some groups seize on human-rights issues, for example, or what they deem to be egregiously inappropriate political arrangements in other nations. An especially prominent case occurred when citizens in many nations labeled the former apartheid policies of South Africa an affront to universal values and emphasized that the South African government was not legitimately representing the interests of a majority of South Africa's residents. Such views caused many national governments to apply economic sanctions against South Africa. Examples of value conflicts are not restricted to human rights, however. Groups focusing on environmental issues characterize tropical rain forests as the lungs of the world and the genetic repository for numerous species of plants and animals that are the heritage of all mankind. Such views lead Europeans, North Americans, or Japanese to challenge the timber-cutting policies of Brazilians and Indonesians. A recent controversy over tuna fishing with long drift nets that kill porpoises is yet another example. Environmentalists in the United States whose sensibilities were offended by the drowning of porpoises required U.S. boats at some additional expense to amend their fishing practices. The U.S. fishermen, complaining about imported tuna caught with less regard for porpoises, persuaded the U.S. government to ban such tuna imports (both direct imports from the countries in which the tuna is caught and indirect imports shipped via third countries). Mexico and Venezuela were the main countries affected by this ban; a GATT dispute panel sided with Mexico against the United States in the controversy, which further upset the U.S. environmental community.

A common feature of all such examples is the existence, real or alleged, of "psychological externalities" or "political failures." Those holding such views reject untrammeled political sovereignty for nation-states in deference to universal or non-national values. They wish to constrain the exercise of individual nations' sovereignties through international negotiations or, if necessary, by even stronger intervention.

The Management of International Convergence

In areas in which arbitrage pressures and cross-border spillovers are weak and psychological or political externalities are largely absent, national governments may encounter few problems with deeper integration. Diversity across nations may persist quite easily. But at the other extreme, arbitrage and spillovers in some areas may be so strong that they threaten to erode national diversity completely. Or psychological and political sensitivities may be asserted too powerfully to be ignored. Governments will then be confronted with serious tensions, and national policies and behaviors may eventually converge to common, worldwide patterns (for example, subject to internationally agreed norms or minimum standards). Eventual convergence across nations, if it occurs, could happen in a harmful way (national policies and practices being driven to a least common denominator with externalities ignored, in effect a "race to the bottom") or it could occur with mutually beneficial results ("survival of the fittest and the best").

Each study in this series addresses basic questions about the management of international convergence: if, when, and how national governments should intervene to try to influence the consequences of arbitrage pressures, cross-border spillovers, diminished autonomy, and the assertion of psychological or political externalities. A wide variety of responses is conceivable. We identify six, which should be regarded not as distinct categories but as ranges along a continuum.

National autonomy defines a situation at one end of the continuum in which national governments make decentralized decisions with little or no consultation and no explicit cooperation. This response represents political sovereignty at its strongest, undiluted by any international management of convergence.

Mutual recognition, like national autonomy, presumes decentralized decisions by national governments and relies on market competition to guide the process of international convergence. Mutual recognition, however, entails exchanges of information and consultations among governments to constrain the formation of national regulations and policies. As understood in discussions of economic integration within the European Community, moreover, mutual recognition entails an explicit acceptance by each member nation of the regulations, standards, and certification procedures of other members. For example, mutual recognition allows wine or liquor produced in any European Union country to be sold in all twelve member countries even if production standards in member countries differ. Doctors licensed in France are permitted to practice in Germany, and vice versa, even if licensing procedures in the two countries differ.

Governments may agree on rules that restrict their freedom to set policy or that promote gradual convergence in the structure of policy. As international consultations and monitoring of compliance with such rules become more important, this situation can be described as *monitored decentralization*. The Group of Seven finance ministers meetings, supplemented by the IMF's surveillance over exchange rate and macroeconomic policies, illustrate this approach to management.

Coordination goes further than mutual recognition and monitored decentralization in acknowledging convergence pressures. It is also more ambitious in promoting intergovernmental cooperation to deal with them. Coordination involves jointly designed mutual adjustments of national policies. In clear-cut cases of coordination, bargaining occurs and governments agree to behave differently from the ways they would have behaved without the agreement. Examples include the World Health Organization's procedures for controlling communicable diseases and the 1987 Montreal Protocol (to a 1985 framework convention) for the protection of stratospheric ozone by reducing emissions of chlorofluorocarbons.

Explicit harmonization, which requires still higher levels of intergovernmental cooperation, may require agreement on regional standards or world standards. Explicit harmonization typically entails still greater departures from decentralization in decisionmaking and still further strengthening of international institutions. The 1988 agreement among major central banks to set minimum standards for the required capital positions of commercial banks (reached through the Committee on Banking Regulations and Supervisory Practices at the Bank for International Settlements) is an example of partially harmonized regulations.

At the opposite end of the spectrum from national autonomy lies *federalist mutual governance*, which implies continuous bargaining and joint, centralized decisionmaking. To make federalist mutual governance work would require greatly strengthened supranational institutions. This end of the management spectrum, now relevant only as an analytical benchmark, is a possible outcome that can be imagined for the middle or late decades of the twenty-first century, possibly even sooner for regional groupings like the European Union.

Overview of the Brookings Project

Despite their growing importance, the issues of deeper economic integration and its competition with national political sovereignty were largely neglected in the 1980s. In 1992 the Brookings Institution initiated its project on Integrating National Economies to direct attention to these important questions.

In studying this topic, Brookings sought and received the co-operation of some of the world's leading economists, political scientists, foreign-policy specialists, and government officials, representing all regions of the world. Although some functional areas require a special focus on European, Japanese, and North American perspectives, at all junctures the goal was to include, in addition, the perspectives of developing nations and the formerly centrally planned economies.

The first phase of the project commissioned the twenty-one scholarly studies listed at the beginning of the book. One or two lead discussants, typically residents of parts of the world other than the area where the author resides, were asked to comment on each study.

Authors enjoyed substantial freedom to design their individual studies, taking due account of the overall themes and goals of the project. The guidelines for the studies requested that at least some of the analysis be carried out with a non-normative perspective. In effect, authors were asked to develop a "baseline" of what might happen in the absence of changed policies or further international cooperation. For their normative analyses, authors were asked to start with an agnostic posture that did not prejudge the net benefits or costs resulting from integration. The project organizers themselves had no presumption about whether national diversity is better or worse than international convergence or about what the individual studies should conclude regarding the desirability of increased integration. On the contrary, each author was asked to address the trade-offs in his or her issue area between diversity and convergence and to locate the area, currently and prospectively, on the spectrum of international management possibilities running between national autonomy through mutual recognition to coordination and explicit harmonization.

HENRY J. AARON   SUSAN M. COLLINS
RALPH C. BRYANT   ROBERT Z. LAWRENCE

Chapter 1

Introduction

Recent decades, and especially recent years, have witnessed a phenomenon of great economic significance, a phenomenon that is having and will continue to have major implications for taxation. This is the growing integration of the world's economies. This process of deepening integration is evidenced and is characterized by several aspects affecting movements across frontiers of goods and services, of financial capital, of factors of production, of technology, and so forth. As tariffs and other restrictions to the movement of goods and services have been reduced or even eliminated, trade among countries has grown considerably faster than their output. Restrictions on the exportation and importation of financial capital have also been progressively removed, stimulating a phenomenal growth in the world capital market and bringing about a considerable reduction in the dispersion in long-term real interest rates across countries. Many countries now allow individuals and institutions to export and import financial capital freely.

Capital movements have been made easier by technological developments, especially in the communication industry and in the use of computers. Information is now more easily and quickly available than in the past and can be sent around the world in seconds. Capital transfers can thus be made in a matter of seconds.

In addition to the freer movement of goods and services and of financial capital, or perhaps as a complement to it, factors of production, as reflected in direct investment, management, labor with a high degree of human capital, and particular technologies, as reflected in patents and in particular ways of producing products, can now cross

1

frontiers much more easily than in the past. This has led to the growth of truly multinational enterprises, whose scope of activity transcends any one country and which can no longer be thought of as enterprises of a particular country.[1]

Multinational enterprises operate their production branches in several countries, trying to exploit various comparative and at times even policy advantages of particular locations. Because of this, integrated international production trade among branches or subsidiaries of the same multinational corporations has been growing very fast and now accounts for a large share of total world trade. More and more international trade reflects trade among various parts of multinational corporations. This has increased the difficulty of allocating the profits of these corporations among the countries where they operate and consequently of taxing those profits.

The developments mentioned above and other similar ones have important implications for policy in general and for tax policy and tax administration in particular. This book focuses on their effect on current and developing tax systems.

Governments generally attempt to cover their public spending through taxation. Reflecting their own specific preferences, different countries are likely to perceive their public expenditure needs differently. Some governments wish to spend more than others. As a consequence, they aim at raising a higher share of national income or of gross domestic product (GDP) in tax revenue. Other governments are satisfied with a lower level of public spending and thus can get along with a smaller tax level.[2]

These preferences are reflected in the countries' shares of tax revenue in the GDP. For industrial countries, these shares now vary from a low of about 30 percent for some countries to a high of more than 50 percent for some others. Tax levels rose considerably and continuously for much of this century, although in recent years, the rate of increase has slowed down or has even become negative for some countries. For developing countries, the shares of taxes in the GDP are lower, reflecting, perhaps, the inability to collect higher tax levels or the greater propensity to influence economic behavior through policies

1. See United Nations (1993).
2. Whether these government preferences reflect the public interest is important, but it is a question not discussed at this point.

other than taxation and public spending.[3] In most developing countries, the share of taxes in the GDP ranges between 10 and 25 percent.

Although there is much disagreement among political groups and among tax experts about the extent to which taxes should be used to bring about some redistribution of income, most governments give, or at least they claim to give, some importance to this objective. For this reason, progressivity in the rates of some important taxes remains prevalent in the countries' tax systems, even though the degree of progressivity reflected in the tax laws has generally fallen in recent years. If countries were compelled to reduce or eliminate this progressivity by international competition, at least some of them would see this as a real political cost.

Rational governments also attempt to minimize the welfare costs that accompany the imposition of taxes. These costs originate from the fact that taxes push or pull individuals and enterprises in directions that may be different from those that would have been chosen in the absence of taxes and, presumably, in the presence of a well-functioning, competitive market.[4] For example, excise taxes change the pattern of consumption of individuals, pushing them away from the choices that, in the absence of externalities, would have maximized their welfare (that is, their consumer surplus).[5] Individuals are likely to increase the consumption of the untaxed goods and decrease that of the taxed goods, thus reducing their total welfare. Taxes on the returns to capital (interests, dividends, profits) change the intertemporal choice of individuals by reducing the net of tax rate of return and thus by making present consumption relatively cheaper than future consumption.[6] Thus individuals are discouraged from saving, and the country's potential rate of growth is reduced. Taxes on work income change the leisure-work choice by making (untaxed) leisure relatively cheaper compared to the utility derived form work (that is, because they reduce the after-tax income, they reduce the utility that the worker obtains from working an extra hour). As a

3. Developing countries make much greater use of regulations to influence economic activities.

4. If the market is not functioning well, second-best considerations arise and the conclusion as to the effect of taxes becomes more tentative.

5. Of course, when externalities are present, taxes may be imposed to improve the allocation of resources. Environmental taxes would be an example.

6. Saving today will generate less consumption in the future than would be the case in the absence of taxes.

consequence, workers may be encouraged to reduce the number of hours spent working unless income effects (that is, the need to maintain a given total after-tax income) do not prevail over the tax-induced substitution effects.

In general, taxes may push individuals toward higher consumption; more leisure; and more untaxed household activities, including do-it-yourself work, subsistence activities, and other activities that can avoid taxation. However, the magnitudes of these effects remain controversial. Empirical evidence has not been able to provide results that were beyond challenge.

The inefficiencies that taxes bring to the economy depend largely on two factors: the level of the tax rates with which tax bases are taxed, and the elasticity of those bases with respect to the tax rates. The lower the tax rate and the more inelastic the tax base, the less effect taxation will have on economic behavior. Within the limits imposed by equity considerations and given their revenue needs, governments that paid some attention to economic efficiency would thus attempt to keep tax rates as low as possible, especially on elastic bases.

The need for the high levels of taxation necessary to support a large social role for the public sector has often required the imposition of high rates even on tax bases with potentially high elasticities.[7] When the level of taxation in a country reaches 30 or 40 or even 50 percent of the GDP, it is difficult to keep tax rates low or limit tax bases to those that are inelastic. Tax administration and equity considerations limit the amount of taxes that could be obtained from these inelastic bases. Furthermore, tax bases that are inelastic in a closed economy can become elastic in an open economy; an example would be taxation of labor when labor can migrate. The need to accommodate the many social needs that confront modern societies has made the revenue objective of overwhelming importance. As a consequence, efficiency considerations have often taken a back seat to this need and to administrative considerations. The tax systems that have come into existence, both in their levels and in their structures, are more the result of political and administrative considerations and of historical developments than of the rational prescriptions of economists. In fact,

---

7. It should be recalled that the expansion of public spending in industrial countries over the decades has been mainly the result of this growing social role. See Tanzi (1986).

there has been a growing gap between the prescriptions of modern tax theory and the reality of the tax systems.

This book picks up some of the general themes introduced in the preface and analyzes them with respect to tax systems. In a world that continues to be organized into nations and in which tax systems are national in scope and there is no international tax authority, what will be the implication of the internationalization of economic activities for those tax systems? How will countries react to cross-border spillovers, to their diminished national authority, and to the challenges to their political sovereignty that deep integration will bring? Will countries recognize the benefits of collaboration or will they try to go it alone? In which areas and for which countries will collaboration be a preferred response? Where will competition be chosen? What will be the consequences of choosing one strategy over the other?

The nine chapters of this book deal separately with issues related to labor income, indirect taxes, and capital income. Chapter 9 draws some general policy conclusions.

Chapter 2

Taxation and
Economic Integration

INTERNATIONALIZATION of economic activity may not change the objectives that governments try to achieve through their tax systems. However, by expanding the scope of economic activities on the part of taxpayers in different countries and by widening the range of their actions, the internationalization of economic activity will introduce the tax systems of foreign countries among the variables that influence the economic decisions of the taxpayers of particular countries. Like tectonic plates grinding against each other, the tax systems of different countries will develop arbitrage pressures created by different tax rates, by differences in the bases that are taxed, by different possibilities of avoidance and evasion, and so forth. These pressures will be strong in some areas and less strong in some others and will become more intense as the process of world integration proceeds. These pressures will be exploited by private economic operators to improve their economic welfare thus affecting tax revenue, economic efficiency, and the equity of the tax system. In some cases, they may also be exploited by some governments to gain tax revenue or other advantages at the expense of other governments.

The process of internationalization of economic activities will affect taxable bases and will as a consequence force some countries to take a close look, either individually or collectively, at the changes needed to prevent the migration of their taxable capacity to other jurisdictions. It may become difficult to impose some taxes on a country-by-country basis when the countries act independently. This process will force some countries to unilaterally adjust the rates at which they tax particular bases when these rates are much out of line with those of other countries. Or it may force countries to rely more on particular tax bases and less on others; in other words, it may force them to modify their tax structure. In still other cases, groups of countries may jointly recognize the necessity of taking collective actions aimed either at coordinating their tax policy actions, thus explicitly recognizing that these actions may have significant economic effects on other countries, or at attempting to maintain their tax systems by increasing the exchange of information among tax administrations to reduce the possibility that taxpayers use the process of internationalization of economic activities to reduce their tax liabilities through tax avoidance or tax evasion, or even harmonizing their tax systems to reduce arbitrage possibilities and to close tax avoiding holes that may exist.

Thus adaptation, competition, coordination, and harmonization will be the key elements in this process. In the first two of these elements, countries will operate in their individual capacities trying to minimize the cost or maximize the advantage that global integration will bring. In this case, beggar-thy-neighbor policies may be occasionally followed, and a process of "fiscal degradation" may follow. This process is likely to especially hurt countries that start with high tax ratios. How one assesses the final outcome of this process may well depend on the political bias of the observer.[1] Individuals with strong preferences for low tax rates and low levels of taxation, that is, individuals who prefer a smaller social role for the public sector or those who believe that much public spending is wasteful and unproductive, are likely to welcome some of the results of this process. Some economists have argued that political forces and unwise governments have pushed tax rates to levels well beyond what can be considered optimal from an efficiency point of view or from a libertarian political point of view. They argue that these rates damage economic performance, thus reducing the standard of living of future generations, and, perhaps more important, limit economic freedom.[2] Still other economists have argued that current rates may be non-

1. Equally true, what may be "fiscal degradation" for one may be desirable tax reform for another.

2. Many economists associated with the public choice school of thought would reflect this point of view. These economists would support constitutional amendments that impose limits on tax rates.

optimal even from a revenue point of view, so that a reduction in these rates would increase revenue.

Individuals who favor a significant social role for the public sector are likely to be wary about a process that may force rate reductions. They may think that the equilibrium in the tax system brought about by a free and democratic political process is, in a sense, optimal, so that foreign countries should not determine how much a country should collect in taxes or spend collectively. These individuals may prefer a course of action that minimizes competition and adaption and may favor coordination and harmonization, as long as the net result of this process reflects their preferences as to the level of taxation and the structure of the tax system.

Coordination can come in different ways. It can come in an informal way, through occasional or even regular contacts among tax officials of different countries who exchange information about planned reforms, attempt to solve ongoing problems, and try to establish rules for the exchange of information on taxpayers to reduce tax evasion and tax avoidance. Or it can come in more formal ways, through meetings in which high-level countries' representatives announce the tax reforms that these countries plan to introduce and try to avoid tax changes that may negatively affect other countries.

Some form of tax coordination among countries is carried out by the Committee on Fiscal Affairs of the Organization for Economic Cooperation and Development (OECD). This committee meets twice a year in Paris.[3] It is attended by representatives of the tax offices of all of the OECD countries.[4] The United States is represented by officials of the Internal Revenue Service and the U.S. Treasury. These meetings help the officials of these countries to keep in touch with each other's thinking, to exchange information, and to develop joint positions on particular technical issues. They allow them to deal with particular technical problems that may arise.[5] These exchanges have great value. However, they cannot perform a fully coordinating role with respect to major tax reforms.[6]

---

3. Some of the working groups reporting to this committee may meet more often.

4. Some other countries and a few international institutions also participate as observers.

5. Another useful forum for the Western Hemisphere and several other countries is the Inter-American Center for Tax Administration (CIAT).

6. Some of the thinking that has guided the work of the Committee on Fiscal Affairs can be found in Messere (1993).

First, representation on the Committee of Fiscal Affairs is limited to OECD countries. Thus although all industrial countries are represented, many countries are not. Second, the individuals who attend these meetings are not the most senior individuals responsible for tax "reform" as compared to tax administration. They are not the ministers of finance of the countries, although, of course, those who attend are supposed to represent those ministers. Third, unlike monetary policy, which is made by a few individuals who have the full power to make the changes, tax policy and tax reform must have the approval of parliaments, so it is not clear who, for example, could commit the United States to an agreement on a major tax reform in an international meeting.[7]

There is no formal international institution representing all countries that plays a role in the tax area similar to that played by the General Agreement on Tariffs and Trade (GATT) in the trade area or by the International Monetary Fund on exchange rate policy. As a consequence, there has never been a formal attempt at coordinating tax policies in the same way that, say, the GATT has been responsible for carrying through the principles agreed to by the Uruguay Round. In any case, unlike trade, for which the obvious reference point is free trade, it would be very difficult to agree on the instructions to give to such an agency.

The lack of such an agency and the difficulty of agreeing on a mandate that could be given one if it came into existence make it obvious how difficult it would be to proceed on the way to tax harmonization, a process by which countries would agree on tax systems with equal rates and bases for relevant taxes. In any case, the need for tax harmonization is not obvious and the case for it is not easy. Even the European Union has not been very successful in pushing forward the process of tax harmonization in its member countries.

In a deeply integrating world,

—Consumption is no longer limited to the country where the taxpayer resides. A country may be tempted to and able to attract consumers from other countries and might be able to tax them, thus increasing its tax revenue. Or the country may lose revenue if its citizens can shop in countries with lower tax rates and can bring the

7. For a discussion of this point, see Tanzi (1989).

purchased commodities to their own country without paying additional taxes. Open frontiers would facilitate this process.

—A country's factors of production (capital and, to a lesser extent, labor) may be pushed out of the country if they are subjected to relatively high tax rates not compensated by better public services provided by the residence country.

—The residents of the country may find investing their financial savings abroad advantageous if this somehow reduces the tax rate on the return to those savings, perhaps by facilitating the underreporting of their incomes.

These and other possibilities are discussed in the rest of this book, focusing particularly on the effect of globalization on *tax revenue, economic efficiency,* and *equity.* The implication of globalization for tax administration and, to a much lesser extent, for stabilization also receives some attention. The discussion identifies differences in tax systems that can continue to exist in the face of the growing integration of the world economies and differences that cannot continue and that somehow must be reconciled.

The barriers to the movement of individuals, goods, services, and capital can be physical, technical, cultural, regulation-based, and fiscal. This book focuses on the fiscal barriers. Still, a few words can be said about nontax obstacles to deep integration.

In most countries, there are still major obstacles to the movement of individuals across international boundaries. Visas are often required to visit countries; hard-to-get special permits are required to work in a foreign country; and other major obstacles still remain that prevent migration to most countries.[8] However, highly skilled individuals with unusual or highly valuable human capital seem to have far less difficulty in moving than most individuals. This aspect may have some important implications for taxation that are discussed later. In other words, it is the taxation of the relatively few but highly mobile individuals rather than the relatively immobile labor that should receive particular attention.[9] Taxation theory has overplayed the assumed immobility of labor.

---

8. For example, the accreditation of diplomas, degrees, and other qualifications remains a major obstacle to the movement of labor.

9. For example, in the United States a large proportion of graduate students in scientifically related fields come from countries from which it would be difficult for a normal laborer to get visas to the United States (China, India, Korea). Many of these students never go back to their native countries, and somehow they manage to get work permits and visas. This brain drain has become a major concern to China.

Barriers to the movement of goods across nations have been falling, especially across nations belonging to free-trade areas such as the European Union. They will also be falling in North American Free Trade Agreement (NAFTA) countries. For most products, import duties are now relatively low in industrial countries where foreign trade taxes have become an insignificant share of total tax revenue.[10] In developing countries, however, foreign trade taxes continue to generate large revenues despite recent lowering of tariffs in many of them.[11] However, other obstacles—quotas, health and environmental regulations, obstacles of a cultural nature—remain. Thus the process of trade liberalization is far from complete.

The barriers to the provision of services across countries—and especially of banking, insurance, air transportation, telecommunication—remain significant and have been the subject of close attention on the part of the GATT and of particular governments. Although tax considerations play a role in this context, that role is likely to be secondary compared to that played by regulations and by specific legislation that often forbid foreigners to operate within a given country—as, for example, in air transportation. This aspect is not addressed in this book.

The process of capital liberalization has perhaps gone furthest. As Adam Smith already recognized 200 years ago, capital was never the citizen of any country. However, there are far fewer obstacles to its movement now than was the case in the past. *Financial* capital can now be shifted across countries and especially across industrial countries almost without any barriers. Technological developments have facilitated this process. At the same time, obstacles to *direct* investment have also become somewhat less significant except in particularly sensitive areas such as defense and transportation.[12] It is especially with respect to capital liberalization that many interesting tax issues arise.

As discussed previously, taxes often distort the allocation of resources and impose deadweight losses on the economy. These distortions may come in the choice by consumers among products, in the choice by producers among factors of production, in the choice by

10. Frenkel, Razin, and Sadka (1991, p. 212) have reported that "between 1950 and 1980, the average tariff rate in the industrial countries fell from about 40 percent to less than 5 percent."

11. In these countries, foreign trade taxes generate about one-third of total tax revenue.

12. See Tanzi and Coelho (1991).

workers between work and leisure, in the choice by savers between consumption and saving, and in several other ways.

A tax incentive to an activity not given in compensation for a positive externality generated by that activity generally attracts more resources to that activity than would be the case in the absence of the subsidy. If resources had been optimally allocated, the overexpansion of the activity reduces general welfare. By the same token, a subsidy given through the budget to the same activity would do the same. A tax disincentive will do the opposite by driving resources away from that activity. These effects occur whether an economy is closed or open. However, economic integration adds other dimensions to the problem.

The integration of economies, and especially the internationalization of financial markets that provides access to the international capital market, may significantly increase the welfare costs associated with tax-induced distortions compared to what they would be in a closed economy. The reason for this important conclusion is, perhaps, obvious, but its importance is not commonly appreciated. When borrowing is not restricted by national frontiers and legal obstacles, a distortion in the form of a tax incentive to an investment category (say, manufacturing or housing) can attract, and is likely to attract, more capital to it than would be the case in closed economies. This occurs because the internationalization of the capital market raises the elasticity of the supply of funds to the economy so that the additional investment is not as quickly discouraged by an increasing supply of credit as it would be in a closed economy.[13] Of course, a distortion that reduces the after-tax rate of return to an investment reduces investment by more than would be the case in closed economies because the funds can more easily be invested abroad at the prevailing world rate of return.[14] These effects are much stronger for smaller than for larger economies.

Even in the absence of distortions associated with particular incentives, economic integration and capital liberalization on a global basis imply that the playing field across countries, at least for particular taxes, must be leveled; otherwise, tax differences across countries will induce capital movements and potentially large dis-

13. In a closed economy, investment is constrained by the much more limited availability of savings. In an open economy, it is not.

14. For a rigorous proof of this proposition, see Bovenberg (1986).

Figure 2-1. *Effect of Internationalization on Elasticity of a Tax Base*

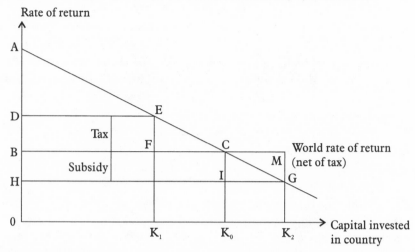

Source: Adapted from Centre for Economic Policy Research (1993, p. 78).

tortions, thus reducing the efficiency with which the world allocates its resources.

The internationalization of markets does not have the same effect on the elasticity of all tax bases. It will have large effects on some (financial capital), marginal or no effects on others (land, already installed capital, unskilled labor), and intermediate effects on others (skilled labor). The greater the effect of internationalization on the elasticity of a tax base, the greater the distortions created by differences in effective tax rates across countries and thus the greater the cost for a country in maintaining its tax rate above those of other countries. This point is shown vividly in figure 2-1.

In figure 2-1, it is assumed that capital is perfectly mobile while labor is immobile. Thus all the labor available is combined with the capital invested. The horizontal axis measures the quantity of capital invested in a given (small) country. The return to capital is measured on the vertical axis. Given a fixed immobile supply of labor, the return to capital investment falls (and the return to labor rises) as more capital is invested in the country. This is shown by the AG schedule, which is the demand for capital schedule. BM is the perfectly elastic world supply of capital. OB (or K_0C) is the net-of-tax international rate of return to capital. This is the rate that investors need to earn to keep their capital in the country. It is also the rate at which investors can borrow any capital they want from the international capital market. A rate of return lower than OB will induce capital to leave the country.

In the absence of capital taxation or of capital subsidies, the amount of capital invested in the country will be OK_0. At point C, the demand for and the supply of capital intersect. The total capital invested will earn an income equivalent to the OK_0CB area. The residual income, the triangle BCA, will compensate the immobile factors of production, including labor.

If the country imposes a tax on capital equal to BD (or FE), an amount of capital equal to K_1K_0 will leave the country because only an amount of capital investment equal to OK_1 can still earn a net-of-tax rate of return equivalent to the world rate of return. Of the total new income, that is, OK_1EA, OK_1FB is the share of capital net of tax, BFED is tax revenue, and DEA is the return to other factors of production, including labor. It is obvious that labor is now worse off. In a world with perfect capital mobility a tax on capital, imposed by a given country, will fall on the immobile factor, assumed to be labor. The capital that leaves the country K_1K_0 will, of course, earn income equal to K_1K_0CF abroad.

Several important conclusions fall from this example. First, there is a net welfare loss to the country (and to the world) associated with taxation of capital at a different rate from that imposed in other countries because the income represented by the triangle FCE is lost: The immobile factors get DEA; the government gets BFED; and the capital that has migrated earns K_1K_2CF; but nobody gets the area covered by the FCE triangle. Second, although the tax has been imposed on capital, the immobile factors bear the burden of the net welfare loss, FCE, even if the government spends its tax revenue, BFED, for their benefits. Third, it may thus become impossible to tax capital and labor equally, as is done with a global income tax, unless all countries do so. Finally, given that the supply of funds is perfectly elastic, the effect of a tax on capital movements will depend on the slope of the demand for capital, that is, on the slope of schedule AG.

Figure 2-1 can also be used to show the effect on world welfare if a country subsidizes investment at a rate equal to BH. In this case, an amount of capital equal to K_0K_2 will be attracted to the country. This capital will be paid an income equal to K_0K_2MC, but it will only generate a value equal to K_0K_2GC. Thus the world welfare will be reduced by an amount equal to the triangle GMC.

Financial markets have become global and countries' economies have become more integrated if for no other reason than for the effect of trade liberalization and the growing role of transnational corporations. Corporations with plants in different countries, and that can borrow internationally, are likely to be particularly sensitive to the tax advantages of one location over another. As a consequence, investment behavior has become more sensitive with respect to tax incentives and to tax differences across countries.[15] With increased movement of financial capital and the growing role of multinational corporations, the need for leveling the tax field internationally must have grown from the time when the countries' economies were relatively closed. Without such a leveling, easier capital movements will more quickly equate the after-tax rates of return. Such equalization will, of course, imply an excessive investment in countries with lower effective tax rates and will thus reduce the efficiency with which world capital is allocated.

As an example of this sensitivity, Hans-Werner Sinn has argued in several papers that the drastic reduction in the taxes on capital introduced in 1981 by the Reagan administration pulled a lot of foreign capital into the United States because the tax reform, by providing what amounted to an immediate write-off for capital investment, raised the net-of-tax rate of return to capital in the United States above the level in other countries. This policy eventually led to an appreciation of the dollar and, according to Sinn, to a major misallocation of the world capital. Capital went to the United States because capital taxes were low and not because the real rate of return to capital was higher. Thus the capital attracted to the United States may have been pulled away from investments in other countries where it would have had a higher (pretax) rate of return. Sinn has claimed that "a conservative estimate of the long-run U.S. capital import resulting from [the Accelerated Cost Recovery System] was $1 trillion."[16] Such a large figure would have implied a major misallocation of the world capital and a reduction of the world's rate of growth.

15. For some evidence based on a survey of 173 large U.K. companies, see Devereux and Pearson (1989).
16. See Sinn (1989, p. 153).

In the situation described above, the possibility that tax instruments may replace other instruments (such as capital restrictions, exchange rates, monetary policy) as tools of economic policy must not be discounted. For example, a couple of years ago Argentine policymakers attempted to compensate for the effect of an appreciating real exchange rate through the reduction of some taxes on actual and potential exporters.[17] In OECD circles, there has been concern that this situation will lead some countries to shift tax bases artificially from other countries to themselves by "unfairly" lowering relevant tax rates. This possibility is particularly relevant for capital taxation. This situation could damage existing tax systems and lead to what is sometimes called fiscal degradation.

17. There is now much interest in the effect of taxes on the competitiveness of nations.

Chapter 3

Lessons from the
American Experience

A PROCESS of deep integration that achieved its ultimate limit would be characterized by a situation in which individuals, capital, and goods could cross frontiers without any impediment. An economic area that shows these characteristics to the extreme is the United States. In this federation, local jurisdictions (states, municipalities, counties) have their own tax systems, but the individuals living in them can work, make purchases, invest, and engage in any legitimate economic activity in any state, county, or municipality they choose. As a consequence, the United States can provide valuable lessons for the ongoing process of economic integration throughout the world.

The states, and to some extent the counties and municipalities, can be visualized as separate countries pursuing independent but necessarily interrelated tax policies. These localities could pursue totally autarchic tax policies, thus ignoring their neighbors, but they would be constrained in their actions by the likely reactions of neighboring governments to some of their actions and by the behavior of their taxpayers who might try to exploit to their advantage the differences that exist among the tax systems of the different states.

If all taxes were personal and benefit taxes, in the sense that all the taxes collected from individuals were based on their incomes and the proceeds from these taxes were spent for services that benefited those same individuals, tax differences across states might not matter very much. Individuals who paid more taxes would receive more benefits and thus would not think that they were worse off. However, even if all taxes were spent for the direct benefits of taxpayers as a group (say, for schools, health, roads, police protection), given the different characteristics of taxpayers (some with children, some without; some young, some old), some individuals would still benefit more than other individuals. Furthermore, most governments use part of their tax revenue for redistributive purposes so that some individuals benefit at the cost of others. Also, many taxes are not personal but are collected from transactions and income flows. These taxes give the taxpayers the possibility of being free riders if they can reduce their tax burden without being affected on the benefits they receive from the government. For all these reasons, taxpayers would find it to their advantage if they could reduce their tax burdens. Cross-border transactions and cross-border income flows create arbitrage pressures and opportunities for tax avoidance as long as the tax systems of different jurisdictions diverge significantly. These pressures cannot be ignored by the policymakers.

If one state imposed taxes on consumption that were much higher than those imposed by other, and especially neighboring, states, the individuals living in that state would be encouraged to shop in other states, thus contributing to the tax revenue of other states. This would happen even if the state spent all its tax revenue for services that benefited the community. In other words, the free rider problem would be present.

If the state imposed much higher taxes on labor income than other states, some individuals might be tempted to move to the other states unless the higher public expenditure in the former compensated them for the higher taxes. If taxes on capital income were higher, savers would have an incentive to invest their savings in states with lower taxes unless the state in which they reside required, as, in fact, all states do, that the tax payment be made to it *and* provided that it were able to get the relevant information on the incomes earned out of state to tax its residents effectively.

If the state imposed higher taxes on enterprises than other states, it would encourage at least some enterprises to establish themselves in states with lower taxes unless it offers advantages in terms of social, physical, and legal environment, public services, amenities, quality of the work force, and so forth that neutralize the difference in tax burden. A low tax environment is, of course, not necessarily a preferred environment.

Tax differences are important. However, it is easy to exaggerate their effect. Individuals and perhaps even enterprises usually have a preferred habitat, which is often the place they have been living in and to which they have become accustomed. Furthermore, a full knowledge of the environment, a knowledge acquired from having resided there for a long time, often involves a lowering of costs because that knowledge implies that the least-cost options within that habitat are known and have been exploited.[1] To individuals, in particular, mobility may impose considerable costs that may be monetary but, more important, psychological or social. These costs are much lower for movements within the United States than for movements from one country to another, especially when the language is different.[2] All this means that *small* tax differences may not be sufficient to induce behavioral changes when the costs mentioned above are significant. Those who live in Washington, D.C., will not go to Alaska for shopping because there is no general sales tax and will not move to that state because it does not have an income tax.[3]

However, deep integration and new technologies may create opportunities that can be exploited at particularly low costs. These opportunities are likely to be especially important in the taxation of financial capital, but they begin to exist more and more also in the taxation of consumption. For example, mail-order purchases are becoming more important not only within the United States but also across countries.[4] Those who have traveled in foreign countries in recent years must have noticed the increasing frequency of advertisement of products in the CNN programs. These advertisements are not aimed at the citizens of a specific country but at the citizens of the world. These products can be ordered by telephone or by mail from particular countries and can be paid for by using a common credit card. The use of a credit card and a telephone is often sufficient to make purchases across frontiers.

1. Of course, having been in one place for a long time may also bring about rigidities and costs, such as the unwillingness of the enterprise to reduce the work force or to close inefficient plants.

2. This may explain why the Tiebout hypothesis, which assumes that people vote with their feet by moving to jurisdictions where the pattern of taxes and public spending is closer to their preferences, is more readily accepted by American economists than by European economists. For a devastating criticism of that hypothesis, see Bewley (1981).

3. Alaska repealed its individual income tax in 1979 and does not have a general sales tax.

4. The Economic Commission has been paying some attention to this issue. For the United States, see Duncan (1988).

Clearly, the world and, of course, the states of the United States must be becoming progressively more sensitive to tax differences. Or putting it differently, differentials in tax rates that may not have been significant in the past may become important in the future as new technologies allow individuals to exploit them at low costs. These developments are likely to force some countries to reduce their tax rates if these are significantly higher than those of other countries.

In the United States, the states are similar to very open economies, operating in an environment of completely free trade, no border controls, and complete capital and labor mobility. In other words, they represent an extreme version of where deep integration of the world economies might lead. For this reason the American experience is of particular interest.

Table 3-1 presents information on the rates of major taxes imposed by states. The table includes information on individual income taxes, corporation income taxes, general sales taxes, and excise taxes on gasoline and cigarettes. The main objective of the table is to show the rate differences that are tolerated by the American states. Obviously, some arbitrage pressures must arise from the differences in the rates and from the costs to the taxpayers in exploiting these differences. If the costs in exploiting these differences are high, larger rate differentials are likely to be tolerated and to have less effect on economic decisions.

Table 3-1 shows that for *individual income taxes* there are differences as large as 12 percentage points (for the marginal tax rates) between the states that do not have a tax on the income of individuals (Alaska, Florida, Nevada, South Dakota, Texas, Washington, and Wyoming) and Massachusetts, the state with the highest marginal tax rate. Other states with relatively high rates are California, Hawaii, Iowa, Maine, Montana, Oregon, and a few others. In many places, individuals are also taxed by municipal or county taxes, generally with somewhat lower rates.

The rates reported in table 3-1 exaggerate somewhat the arbitrage pressures created by taxes on individual income. First, they represent marginal and not average tax rates. The average tax rates, expressed as a percentage of personal income, in 1991 ranged from zero to more than 4 percent in the District of Columbia, Maryland, New York, and Oregon, with a national average of 2.4 percent.[5] Second, because of

5. Advisory Commission on Intergovernmental Relations (1993b, pp. 96–97).

Table 3-1. *Rates of Major State Taxes, 1992*
Percent unless otherwise specified

State	Individual income tax (range)	Corporation income tax (range)	General sales taxes	Gasoline ($/gallon)	Cigarettes ($/pack)
Alabama	2.0–5.0	5.0	4.0	0.16	0.165
Alaska	0.0	1.0–9.4	0.0	0.08	0.29
Arizona	3.8–7.0	9.3	5.0	0.18	0.18
Arkansas	1.0–7.0	1.0–6.5	4.5	0.185	0.22
California	1.0–11.0	9.3	6.0	0.16	0.35
Colorado	a	5.0–5.1	3.0	0.22	0.20
Connecticut	4.5[b]	11.5	6.0	0.26	0.45
Delaware	3.2–7.7	8.7	0.0	0.19	0.24
District of Columbia	6.0–9.5	10.0	6.0	0.20	0.50
Florida	0.0	5.5	6.0	0.04	0.339
Georgia	1.0–6.0	6.0	4.0	0.075	0.12
Hawaii	2.0–10.0	4.4–6.4[c]	4.0	0.16	0.40
Idaho	2.0–8.2	8.0	5.0	0.22	0.18
Illinois	3.0	4.8	6.25	0.19	0.30
Indiana	3.4[b]	3.4–4.5	5.0	0.15	0.155
Iowa	0.4–9.98	6.0–12.0	5.0	0.20	0.36
Kansas	4.4–7.75	4.0–7.35	4.9	0.18	0.24
Kentucky	2.0–6.0	4.0–8.25	6.0	0.15	0.03
Louisiana	2.0–6.0	4.0–8.0	4.0	0.20	0.20
Maine	2.1–9.89	3.5–8.93	6.0	0.19	0.37
Maryland	2.0–6.0	7.0	5.0	0.235	0.36
Massachusetts	5.95–12.0	d	5.0	0.21	0.26
Michigan	4.6	d	4.0	0.15	0.25
Minnesota	6.0–8.5	9.8	6.0	0.20	0.48
Mississippi	3.0–5.0	3.0–5.0	7.0	0.18	0.18
Missouri	1.5–6.0	5.0–6.5	4.225	0.13	0.13
Montana	2.0–11.0	6.75	0.0	0.20	0.18
Nebraska	2.37–6.92	5.58–7.81	5.0	0.234	0.27
Nevada	0.0	0.0	6.5	0.225	0.35
New Hampshire	e	8.0	0.0	0.18	0.25
New Jersey	2.0–7.0	9.0	6.0	0.105	0.40
New Mexico	1.8–8.5	4.8–7.6	5.0	0.16	0.15
New York	4.0–7.875	9.0	4.0	0.08	0.39
North Carolina	6.0–7.75	7.75	4.0	0.223	0.05
North Dakota	f	3.0–10.5	5.0	0.17	0.29
Ohio	0.743–6.9	5.1–8.9	5.0	0.21	0.18

(*Table continued on next page*)

Table 3-1. (*continued*)

State	Individual income tax (range)	Corporation income tax (range)	General sales taxes	Gasoline ($/gallon)	Cigarettes ($/pack)
Oklahoma	0.5–7.0	6.0	4.5	0.16	0.23
Oregon	5.0–9.0	6.6	0.0	0.22	0.28
Pennsylvania	2.95	12.25	6.0	0.12	0.31
Rhode Island	g	9.0	7.0	0.26	0.37
South Carolina	2.5–7.0	5.0	5.0	0.16	0.07
South Dakota	0.0	0.0	4.0	0.18	0.23
Tennessee	e	6.0	6.0	0.20	0.13
Texas	0.0	0.0	6.25	0.20	0.41
Utah	2.55–7.2	5.0	5.0	0.19	0.23
Vermont	h	5.5–8.25	5.0	0.15	0.20
Virginia	2.0–5.75	6.0	3.5	0.175	0.025
Washington	0.0	0.0	6.5	0.23	0.34
West Virginia	3.0–6.5	9.075	6.0	0.155	0.17
Wisconsin	4.9–6.93	7.9	5.0	0.222	0.38
Wyoming	0.0	0.0	3.0	0.09	0.12

Source: Adapted by author from various tables in Advisory Commission on Intergovernmental Relations (1993a).

a. 5 percent of federal taxable income.

b. Percent of modified federal adjusted gross income.

c. Financial institutions pay 7.92 percent.

d. Alternative taxes paid.

e. Limited tax.

f. 14 percent of federal tax liability.

g. 27.5 percent of federal tax liability.

h. 28–34 percent of federal tax liability.

the fact that state and local income taxes are deductible from income in the determination of federal income tax liability, even the effective marginal tax rates are somewhat lower than they are reported in the table. In fact, the effective rates would be reduced by about one-third. Third, the free exchange of information between state and federal tax authorities reduces or eliminates the arbitrage possibilities created by tax avoidance or tax evasion behavior.

It is not clear to what extent the differences in the tax rates reported above may have induced some individuals to move from high-taxed to low-taxed states.[6] As already indicated, many other

6. However, as shown below, they may have induced some individuals or some enterprises *not* to move to high-taxed states.

factors enter into the decision of where to live, including the social environment and the availability of good jobs. There is no empirical evidence that indicates that these rate differentials have had much of an effect in pushing individuals out of high-taxed states. But there is evidence to indicate that states have been sensitive to differences in tax rates. For example, it has been argued that the 1986 federal tax reform, by reducing the federal tax rate, increased the spread in the states' effective marginal tax rates and prompted them to cut their own top income tax rates in 1987 and 1988.[7]

In the absence of the free exchange of information among tax authorities, even tax rate differences as low as those reported in the table could induce substantial movements of financial capital from highly taxed to low-taxed jurisdictions to avoid paying higher tax rates. However, the states where the investors reside have full access to the information reported by the taxpayers to the federal authorities. Because of this easy access to information on the incomes from financial investments received from states other than the one where the taxpayer resides, states can enforce a nationwide concept of taxable income. They can thus implement a residence-based principle. As is seen later, this situation is dramatically different from that prevailing in the world at large. In the United States, no withholding taxes are levied on the income flows across different jurisdictions.

The rate differences are also significant for the marginal *income taxes on corporations,* which can range from zero for a few states (Nevada, South Dakota, Texas, Washington, and Wyoming) to 10 percent or slightly higher in others (Connecticut, the District of Columbia, Iowa, North Dakota, and Pennsylvania). At first sight, such large differences for taxes on corporate income are somewhat surprising because one would expect that corporations would react to such differences more vigorously than individuals, thus forcing the states to harmonize the rates.[8] In other words, one would expect that investors would choose to locate in states where these taxes are low.[9]

For the state taxes on corporations, some considerations similar to those mentioned above for individuals also prevail. First, the corpo-

7. See Tannenwald (1991).
8. See McLure (1986b).
9. Over the years, the share of corporate income tax revenue in total corporate profits has generally been rising for states whereas it has generally fallen for the federal government. See Galginaitis (1992).

rate income taxes paid to the states are deductible for determining the federal income tax liability so that the *effective* tax rates are reduced by about one-third. Second, the rate differences mentioned above refer to *marginal* rather than *average* tax rates; some states impose these taxes with progressive rates. Third, many states provide tax incentives and generous deductions that may substantially reduce the burden of high rates.[10] In fact, in 1991 the revenue from state and local corporate income taxes ranged from zero to 2.2 percent of the states' personal income, with a national average of only 0.5 percent of personal income.

Even though the taxes imposed by state and local governments on corporations are not very high, given the facility with which enterprises and capital can move within the United States one would expect that these taxes would play some role in location decisions, even recognizing that other factors besides taxes may be more important. This has been recognized by many theoretical studies.[11] Surveys have often reported that business taxes play a marginal role at best in location decisions. Corporate managers mention them but never prominently, and other factors are always given more importance.[12] Econometric studies, for the most part, have not done much better.[13] However, recent work by Leslie E. Papke and by James R. Hines, Jr., has found stronger effects than in the past.

Papke's work, reported in two recent articles, introduces several technical innovations with respect to earlier work. These innovations are supposed to permit easier assessment of the effect of taxation than was possible with less sophisticated methods. Papke finds that "economic factors do play a significant role in manufacturing location." Furthermore, "industries differ markedly in their responsiveness to variations in state economic characteristics." The author concludes that "state and local governments continue to be sensitive to their level of business taxes; these results indicate that tax composition will have some effect on the composition of industry within the state."[14]

Hines attempts to estimate whether the location of foreign direct investment in the United States is influenced by the state tax rates. To

10. For a survey of tax incentives given by states, see Ledebur and Hamilton (1986).
11. See, for example, Gordon (1983).
12. See Kieschnick (1981).
13. For a review of many of these studies, see Wasylenko (1991).
14. Papke (1991, p. 65); see also Papke (1987).

do this, he separates foreign investors in two groups: those from countries that provide home-country credits for the income taxes paid in the United States, and those from countries that do not allow such a credit. He assumes that the former would not be affected by the state taxes paid whereas the latter would be. Therefore, different investment behavior by these two groups would provide evidence that state taxes do, in fact, play a role in the location decisions of investors. His empirical analysis leads him to conclude that "high state tax rates have a significant negative effect on local investment. Investors who cannot claim credit [in their own countries] for state tax payments appear to reduce their investment shares, relative to foreign tax credit investors, by about 7–9 percent, for every 1 percent rate of taxation."[15]

Thus the state corporate income taxes may influence the location decisions of investors.[16] This may explain why tax rates and tax incentives continue to be important tools for pursuing the objectives of state governments and why states compete for business investment with low rates and with tax incentives. This competition may drive down the statutory or the effective rates in some states, thus forcing other states to do the same or creating conditions for an inefficient spatial allocation of investment. In the process, the allocation of tax revenue is changed and the level of taxation at the state level is reduced. If this process brings some tax rate harmonization, it is a spontaneous result rather than a coordinated policy.

A problem that could have been very serious in connection with the state corporate income taxes is the allocation among the states of income generated by companies that operate in several states. Given that the tax rates are different, that the tax bases are broadly similar, and that the same currency is used for all transactions within the United States, one would expect that, through the use of transfer prices and other "creative accounting" practices, companies would try to transfer to, and thus to show their profits in, states with low or zero corporate income taxes. In this way, they would reduce their aggregate tax liability to the states. Of course, a state's corporate income tax should be levied only on the income generated in that state. However, the determination of that income is very difficult when the enterprises operating in that state have nationwide or even

15. Hines (1993).
16. See also the results obtained by Fox and Murray (1990); and by Bartik (1989).

international activities. To solve this problem, a large majority of the states has adopted some variant of the three-factor "Massachusetts formula."[17] According to this formula, the U.S. taxable income of corporations is allocated to the states in which the corporations operate on the basis of sales, capital assets, and labor income. Each of these factors accounts for one-third of the total weight. In this way, one of the main problems faced by the internationalization of the activities of enterprises is largely (although not totally) solved. Formula apportionment is a far from ideal system for allocating income among jurisdictions and for avoiding double taxation or for avoiding abuses on the part of corporations.

The allocation of corporate income among relevant states carried out by use of formulas is extended to the income of foreign corporations. But some difficulties arise in this connection. The formula is supposed to allocate to a state the income earned in that state to allow the state to tax that income. States are not allowed to tax extraterritorial income. A multinational corporation that operates in several countries and in several states should thus first allocate to the United States the share of world income earned in the United States. It will then allocate the U.S. earnings to the states in which it operates. However, some states (Alaska, California, Montana, and North Dakota) apply formulas based on worldwide corporate income, and the federal government levies the income of companies on a worldwide basis. Some of these issues have created a lot of animosity on the part of foreign countries.[18]

The differences across states in the rates of the *general sales taxes* are smaller than for the taxes on income. The rates of general sales taxes vary from zero in five states (Alaska, Delaware, Montana, New Hampshire, Oregon) to more than 6 percent in six states (Illinois, Mississippi, Nevada, Rhode Island, Texas, Washington). No state imposes sales taxes with rates above 7 percent, and seventeen states impose sales taxes with rates of 6 to 7 percent. Excluding the five states that do not have general sales taxes, all states are in the 3 to 7 percent range, and in fact, most are in the 4 to 6 percent range. These taxes are generally collected from the final consumer in the form of retail sales taxes.

17. Ironically, Massachusetts does not use this formula.
18. For a comprehensive review of the issues that arise when states tax corporations operating in several states, see McLure (1986a).

Some literature in the United States has tried to assess the extent to which differences in tax rates across states (and across countries) induce taxpayers to cross jurisdictional lines for their purchases and thus generate some tax exporting in the sense that some jurisdictions lose tax revenue to their neighbors. One would expect that individuals who are within an easy distance from jurisdictions that impose lower tax rates might take advantage of these differences, that policymakers would be aware of the possibility of distortions in the location of the retail sales and would ensure that tax differentials do not become too large and thus be tempting, and that retailers would be tempted to place their shops close to the border but on the side of the lower-tax jurisdictions. To some extent, all these possibilities are likely to occur, but as is often the case, it has been difficult to quantify their size. Table 3-1 shows that the differentials in tax rates are generally not too high. This may suggest that the states' policymakers have been concerned about the possibility that high tax rates may lead to tax exporting so that some competition-induced tax harmonization has taken place.

Over the years, several experts have attempted to assess the effect of sales taxes on the location of retail sales. For example, John L. Mikesell found that a 1 percent tax rate increase in the center city of 173 standard Metropolitan Statistical Areas would reduce their per capita retail sales by somewhere between 1.69 and 10.97 percent.[19] For the District of Columbia, Ronald C. Fisher found that increases in the sales tax differentials reduced tax revenue from food sales but not from apparel.[20] William F. Fox found that "the sales tax . . . [had] the largest effect on retail activity of any tax, but at the margin tax rate changes would appear to influence only a low percentage of sales." Fox speculates that "selective sales taxes on cigarettes and alcohol may have a greater effect on retail activity."[21] These border effects are more pronounced in contiguous areas along the borders of states, countries, or cities.

Several studies have attempted to estimate the effect of differences in the tax rates on cigarettes on cross-border sales. The latest of these studies, undertaken by KPMG Peat Marwick for the Tax Foundation, found that in contiguous areas with significant excise tax differentials,

19. Mikesell (1970).
20. Fisher (1980).
21. Fox (1986, p. 399).

the loss in tax revenue for the higher-tax jurisdictions can be quite large due to cross-border shopping as well as to smuggling of cigarettes to higher-taxed jurisdictions.[22]

This brief survey of states of the United States, an economic area that characterizes an extreme version of deep integration, is instructive for two reasons. First, it shows the differences in tax rates that are currently tolerated by the governments of the American states. Second, it points to some of the political and economic constraints or costs that accompany economic integration.

There are political constraints when competition forces a jurisdiction to modify the structure of the tax system that it would prefer to have. This change in the structure can leave the jurisdiction with lower tax revenue when competition forces it to lower its tax rates to prevent a loss of its tax bases. Or it can leave it with a different structure when some taxes are more sensitive than others to outside competition. For example, the jurisdiction may be forced to raise the taxes on immobile factors or on products with high transportation costs, and this may conflict with equity considerations. A state that wished to discourage smoking by taxing cigarettes while at the same time wishing to charge smokers for the negative externalities they impose on the community would fail on both counts if smokers could purchase their cigarettes in other states that levied lower taxes on cigarettes. In fact this has happened recently in Canada owing to competition from the United States.

There are economic costs when the tax differentials change economic behavior in a way that reduces welfare. For example, if individuals cross borders to benefit from lower tax rates, say, on sales, but to do so they have to sustain some costs in terms of transportation costs and time lost that they could have avoided by shopping in their own jurisdiction, then the tax differential has reduced welfare. This also happens when an enterprise, because of lower tax rates, chooses a given location over a preferred one purely because of the attraction of a lower tax rate.[23]

However, it must be recognized that by forcing a lowering of the marginal tax rates across jurisdictions, because of tax competition, the process of integration of economies will also bring about some lower-

22. KPMG Peat Marwick (1993).
23. The evidence available from the American states indicates that these economic costs may not be too large, although they do occur.

ing of the welfare costs associated with high marginal tax rates. If a substantial share of public spending is wasteful or unproductive and the lowering of the rates reduces that expenditure, then total welfare gain may be even higher. However, a jurisdiction that could use public resources efficiently and that placed more value on a large role for the government and was unable to pursue that role because of the constraints imposed by the competition from other jurisdictions would think that its net welfare had fallen despite the lowering of the welfare costs of taxation.

The American tax system provides some useful lessons about the implication of deeper integration for the tax system. From the U.S. experience, one might argue that there is no need to coordinate, and even less to harmonize, consumption taxes because competition will ensure that they do not get too much out of line; that there is no need to coordinate local taxes on the incomes of individuals; and that there is also no need to coordinate taxes on enterprises for the same reason as above. However, although useful, the American experience is characterized by features that are specific to it and that thus may reduce its value as a guide to future developments in an integrating world with nation-states, frontiers, different currencies, different legal systems, and different rules and regulations.

First, in the United States the movement of goods across states is not slowed or stopped by quotas, tariffs, health and environmental regulations, and the many explicit and, often more important, implicit obstacles to the flow of goods across countries.[24] In the absence of these obstacles, tax differentials have the potential to play a larger role. The world is still a long way from reaching the American situation despite the significant progress described earlier. As long as this is the case, larger tax differentials than within the United States might not create excessive arbitrage pressures.

Second, in the United States the lack of banking secrecy, and of other obstacles to relatively easy access to information, and the similarity of accounting and legal standards ensure that investors take considerably less risk in investing in a state other than the one where they reside than do foreigners when they invest in other countries. As long as laws related to banking secrecy and to the right to access

24. The European Union is hoping to duplicate this feature, but so far frontiers and different currencies remain obvious reminders that these are still independent nation-states.

information and as long as accounting standards and the quality and veracity of the statements issued by enterprises, banks, investment agents, and so forth are different, the environment for capital movements in the world at large will not be the same as within the United States. Exchange rate risks will also provide an additional obstacle that is absent within the United States. This implies that some tax differences will not lead to the large outflow of capital from higher- to lower-tax countries as assumed by some theoretical studies. Or looking at it from a different angle, it implies that a given difference in tax rates between countries will generate less arbitrage pressure than would be the case within the United States.

Third, and perhaps most important, in the United States more than two-thirds of total taxes are collected by the federal government. These federal taxes are imposed with the same laws, the same rules, and the same administration for every individual and enterprise *in the whole country.* This means that the local taxes, which, in principle, are the ones that raise issues similar to those raised by the ongoing process of integration in the world at large, are a relatively small share of the gross domestic product (GDP). Because of this, the differences in the effective rates with which they are imposed tend to be low and certainly lower than by countries. Furthermore, the information assembled on taxpayers by the federal government, when it collects its income taxes, is available to the states, which, in turn, tend to use the same tax bases as the federal government. This greatly facilitates the collection of taxes at the state level and reduces the question of tax competition mainly to competition of rates rather than competition of bases.[25] It also implies that differences in tax administrations will not be exploited by taxpayers to reduce their tax burden.

Fourth, in the United States, taxes on consumption are either excises on a few goods or general *retail* taxes. The excises are imposed by both the federal government and the states whereas the retail taxes are imposed by the states. Apart from the question of the level of rates, which in the United States tend to be low and thus not very different across states, retail taxes do not create difficulties in a world of deep integration. As long as they are low and as long as they are imposed on *final consumer* goods, they do not distort costs of production or

25. The importance of having uniform tax bases and of having access to information must be kept in mind for later discussion.

trade across countries or even across states.[26] Thus they preserve production efficiency, which is a very important condition for tax neutrality.[27] These conditions, however, do not prevail in the rest of the world, where taxes on consumption are often much higher than in the United States and are often (multistage) value added taxes (VAT). For these taxes, deep integration does raise issues of coordination. One could argue that perhaps VATs should be replaced by retail sales taxes. But most experts agree that it is unwise to impose retail taxes with high rates because such taxes would be difficult to administer, especially in countries with atomized distribution sectors.

Because a retail general sales tax is collected at only one stage (the final stage), it is administratively difficult to use high rates. It is no accident that in the United States in 1992 the highest rate was 7 percent. The VAT, however, being a multistage tax, has some self-enforcing features, so that very high rates are often used. High rates bring about high rate differences. As long as frontiers are in place, these differences do not create difficulties if proper mechanisms remove the tax on exports and add it on imports. However, in a world undergoing a process of deeper integration, frontiers may disappear, thus creating the difficulties now faced by the European Union.

26. A good question is whether these taxes affect the exchange rates.
27. See Diamond and Mirrlees (1971).

Chapter 4

Labor Mobility and Personal Income Taxation

DEEPER integration, together with the growing role of multi-national corporations, can be expected to lead to greater labor mobility; labor would move from activities with low labor productivity to activities with high labor productivity not just within a country but also across countries. Obviously, unrestricted labor mobility is not likely to occur any time soon, and in any case, it might not be totally desirable because of social and political considerations. Large movements of population do generate cultural conflicts and potentially serious social or assimilation problems in the receiving countries. Thus the marginal productivity of labor and, therefore, the level of wages are likely to continue to differ across countries despite the equalization effect brought about by trade, by capital movements, and by changes in the exchange rates. In chapter 2, it was argued that for highly skilled individuals, there is now far more mobility than for the whole population. Some economists have recently argued that these highly skilled individuals may be far more important to growth than is normally assumed. If this is the case, deeper integration may raise some policy concerns for the policymakers of countries that would be the net losers of these individuals. As a consequence, in this chapter, the question is raised as to whether taxation might play a role in these movements, especially in a situation characterized by a continuing process of deeper integration.

The review of the literature dealing with state and local taxation within the United States did not identify any empirical study that strongly concluded that differences in the tax rates on the incomes of individuals had promoted labor movements within the United States despite the fact that the linguistic, cultural, and regulatory obstacles in the United States are not significant. However, several studies found evidence of competition among states in setting marginal tax rates on individuals. One could argue that the income tax rate differences within the United States are not so large as to play a significant role in pushing some individuals out of some states and in pulling them into other states. It should be recalled that among the American states the statutory marginal tax rates range from zero to 12 percent but that because the state income taxes are deductible from adjusted gross income in calculating the federal income taxes, the range is more likely to be at most between zero and about 7 to 8 percent.[1] The *effective average* tax rates are, of course, much lower. The average effective tax rate for state *and local* individual income taxes expressed as a share of personal income was, in fiscal year 1991, 2.4 percent. Four states had a share of more than 4 percent (District of Columbia, Maryland, New York, and Oregon); twelve had a share of more than 3 percent. The top share was New York's, with 4.4 percent.[2]

Despite the relatively low income taxes imposed by local governments, some experts have nevertheless concluded that they may affect labor mobility. For example, Robert Tannenwald has written:

> Regardless of what experts recommend, states often evaluate the competitive standing of their tax system by comparing their highest statutory marginal tax rate on personal income with those of their economic rivals. Proponents of this indicator argue that employers often encounter stiff interstate competition when recruiting managers and other skilled professionals. Because these geographically mobile employees are highly paid, many of them fall within each state's highest income-tax bracket. Managers responsible for the locational decisions of firms generally fall into this tax bracket as well. Consequently, many policymakers believe that they must keep their highest marginal personal income tax rates "in line" with those of rival states to compete for employers and skilled labor.[3]

When we move from a consideration of the individual income taxes within the American local jurisdictions toward those among indepen-

1. That range was even smaller when the marginal federal tax rate was 50 percent (before 1986) and 70 percent (before 1981).
2. Advisory Commission on Intergovernmental Relations (1993b, pp. 96–97).
3. Tannenwald (1991, p. 179).

dent countries, two aspects become significant. First is the increasing importance of various social, linguistic, cultural, and regulatory obstacles that make international movements of labor much more difficult and costly than labor movements within the United States. Second is the potentially much greater importance of income taxes. Whether differences in personal income taxes are measured by statutory marginal tax rates, by average effective tax rates, or in some other way, they loom very large. For example, in 1992 the marginal tax rates ranged from 31 percent in the United States and 33 percent in New Zealand to 65 percent in Japan and 60 percent or more in Denmark, the Netherlands, and Sweden.[4] Many Organization for Economic Cooperation and Development (OECD) countries had marginal tax rates substantially higher than those in the United States.

These differences do not disappear if one considers the effective tax rates. The OECD *Revenue Statistics of OECD Member Countries* shows that in 1991, total personal income taxes as percentages of the gross domestic product (GDP) ranged from 25.8 percent in Denmark to 4.8 percent in Greece, with a weighted average of 11.6 percent for the whole OECD area. Among the G-7 countries, the range was from 15.2 percent in Canada to 6.0 percent in France. Clearly, the pull or the push exercised by the tax systems of some of these countries can be far greater than those generated by the local American governments. In a world undergoing deeper integration, these pressures might be strong enough to overcome the obstacles mentioned earlier and might induce at least some individuals to migrate.[5] Whether these labor movements should be cause for policy attention is clearly an open question. Some concern may be generated by recent analytical work in the spirit of the so-called new growth theory.

In a recent paper, Kevin M. Murphy, Andrei Shleifer, and Robert W. Vishny speculated that the allocation of talent within a country has significant effects on the growth rate of its economy.[6] They highlight the importance that the ablest individuals have for the growth of the

---

4. Organization for Economic Cooperation and Development (1993c). Adding local income taxes to the federal income tax would raise the U.S. marginal tax rates to about 37 to 38 percent. These figures include local income taxes.

5. It would be interesting to see the extent to which these differences may have induced some Canadians to move from the heaviest-taxed Canadian provinces toward the lowest-taxed American states. For these individuals, the differential in marginal tax rates is about 20 percentage points.

6. Murphy, Shleifer, and Vishny (1991).

economy. These individuals introduce new technologies or new ways of doing things and inspire others to institute them. Thus their incomes appropriate only a share of the total effect they have on the economy. Although the number of these individuals may be small, because of the positive externalities they generate, their contribution to economic growth may thus be far larger than indicated by their incomes. However, when the existing incentives within the country in which they live are such that the most talented individuals choose rent-seeking rather than productive careers or activities, the growth rate of the country may be significantly reduced.[7] As they put it,

> When talented people become entrepreneurs, they improve the technology in the line of business they pursue, and as a result, productivity and income grow. In contrast, when they become rent seekers, most of their private returns come from redistribution of wealth from others and not from wealth creation. As a result, talented people do not improve technological opportunities, and the economy stagnates.[8]

These authors argue that individuals with great ability can apply their talent to different fields because basic talent is often not field-specific. Which field talented individuals choose depends on the returns that they expect from the various occupations. Ceteris paribus, they will choose the occupations that offer the highest potential returns (pecuniary and nonpecuniary) to their abilities. Their discussion is conducted in the context of a closed economy; however, in open economies, individuals with great ability have the option of working not only in different fields but also in different countries.[9] Entrepreneurs, inventors, athletes, scientists, artists, and other individuals with great talent often change their country of residence. As evidence of this, consider the national background of many entrepreneurs, tennis stars, great musical performers, scientists, and so forth. This mobility has created the "brain drain" phenomenon that attracted attention a few years ago and that continues to attract "brains" to particular countries.[10] Innovators and individuals with

---

7. Baumol (1990) has made a similar argument.

8. Murphy, Shleifer, and Vishny (1991, p. 505).

9. As mentioned earlier, immigration laws seem to be far less restrictive, de facto, for these individuals than for the average person.

10. This has led to various proposals to tax emigrants. See the papers in Bhagwati and Wilson (1989). American universities are now full of graduate students from China and

great entrepreneurial ability seem to be particularly mobile, as indicated by the considerable number of successful entrepreneurs who were born in other countries.

With few exceptions, recent work on taxation has broadly concluded that, because of the high mobility of capital and the low mobility of labor, taxes on capital income should be low or, in extreme cases, even zero, whereas taxes on labor income need not be low. In other words, it is argued that in open economies the burden of financing the public sector, a burden that is quite substantial in modern economies, should fall mostly on labor and on other immobile factors such as land because, presumably, capital can be invested abroad at zero tax rate. This is a fairly standard conclusion in much of the modern taxation literature.[11] However, the assumption that labor is immobile and thus provides an inelastic or captive tax base is based on the, empirically observed, relatively small proportion of the labor force that can or wants to emigrate. If labor were homogeneous, this argument for defending the assumption of immobility would be acceptable.[12] The relatively small numbers of emigrants would imply that the high taxation of labor income would not induce an increase in the emigration of labor and would thus have an insignificant effect on the rate of growth of the country. However, for the reasons advanced by Murphy, Shleifer, and Vishny, the assumption that labor is homogeneous can be highly misleading and can lead to wrong policies.

Labor income is taxed with progressive rates in most countries. Often, it is the largest component of the base of the global income tax. Because the most talented individuals tend to have the highest incomes, they are often taxed at the highest marginal tax rates, which

---

other countries studying physics and other technical subjects. They often do not go back to their country.

11. See, for example, Auerbach (1985).

12. For a criticism of the view that labor is immobile, see Bird and McLure (1989). Furthermore, it must be recognized that if labor is indeed immobile, it is because of constraints imposed on its potential mobility by laws, regulations, and other obstacles. Frenkel, Razin, and Sadka (1991) have recognized the distinction with respect to international mobility between normal labor and highly skilled labor. They have concluded that "in a world economy with free movements of capital and labor (especially highly skilled labor), the ability of governments to impose a high tax burden on such internationally mobile factors of production, is severely restricted unless a high level of international coordination and tax enforcement is reached among national tax authorities" (pp. 213–14).

can still exceed 60 percent in several countries. If international mobility would allow some of these individuals to avoid these high rates, they will be tempted to emigrate.[13] Newspaper stories have frequently reported such tax-induced migration on the part of well-known and highly talented individuals. Unfortunately, there is no concrete empirical evidence that would allow us to conclude whether this is an empirically significant problem.[14] However, if a significant number of these individuals does move, the cost to a country arising from the high taxation of labor income could be far greater than generally assumed in the literature on taxation. When the emigrants have exceptional talent, even small numbers may imply large losses in terms of growth rates.

Ceteris paribus, the chance that talented individuals will emigrate because of tax considerations will depend on the differential in the taxation of labor income between the country of origin and the country of destination: the higher the differential, the greater the inducement to migrate. For reasons discussed by Murphy, Shleifer, and Vishny, the economic size of the country should also be important.[15] As long as frontiers remain in place, the rate of return to exceptional talent is likely to be higher in a larger than in a smaller country. This implies that small countries with high tax rates on labor income are more likely to experience a serious "brain drain" than larger countries, and especially the United States. It is thus particularly important for small countries to keep their tax rates on labor income low as compared to the United States' to reduce the tax push on their able individuals to emigrate.[16] If a process of deep integration made the frontiers inconsequential, it would reduce but not invalidate the validity of this argument. In such a case, the size of the country would be less important but the tax differentials could become more important.

13. This requires that tax rates on labor income in other countries are lower. In other words, it requires a significant difference in the tax rates. As seen above, this is, in fact, the case.

14. See the tentative conclusions on this issue in Centre for Economic Policy Research (1993, pp. 68–76).

15. Their argument is related to the size of the occupational field. The larger the field, the greater will be the return to ability for those who enter it. In other words, talent is likely to command a higher price in a large rather than in a small field.

16. This argument would be particularly significant for countries such as Canada and Ireland, which are linguistically and perhaps culturally close to the United States.

Taxation theory must identify more explicitly three different factors of production: capital, normal labor, and labor associated with unusual talent. Whether the loss of capital due to capital mobility is more important in determining growth rates than the loss of highly talented individuals due to labor mobility is an empirical question. The arguments discussed above imply that more weight should be given to the mobility of labor than has so far been the case and that tax rates should take this mobility into consideration. Whether tax *policy* and not just tax *theory* can make the required distinction is another matter. For sure, linear taxes on labor income as compared to progressive taxes would, on efficiency grounds, be preferable. But even linear taxes on highly talented individuals can be too high in a world undergoing deep integration and with highly differentiated tax rates.

A conclusion that appears strongly supported by the preceding discussion is that in a market that is becoming progressively more integrated internationally and where legislation or regulations often facilitate the movement of individuals of exceptional talent, high marginal tax rates on personal incomes could influence the choice of these individuals on where they operate. In such a case, the market would observe a movement of the skilled individuals from the high-taxed to the low-taxed areas.[17] If the high-taxed areas are relatively small countries and the low-taxed areas are large countries, the pull and push effect induced by taxation may become larger.

The preceding discussion raises a key question that surfaces in other areas: whether the reference point for assessing the effect of taxation should be the welfare of a specific country or the welfare of the world. If the externality argument about highly talented individuals has some validity and if the talent of these individuals can generate more output in a larger country than in a smaller country, their migration might be welfare-reducing to their country of origin but welfare-enhancing to the country of destination and, by implication, to the world at large. The discussion also raises the question of what can be done to prevent integration from making potential distortions worse. This issue is taken up in later chapters, especially chapter 9.

17. As Joel Slemrod (1990a, p. 33) has put it, "Many of the issues raised by tax havens, tax bargains, and tax addresses apply to labor as well as capital. Individuals may be induced by low rates (relative to services offered) to move their true country of residence, thus taking advantage of a tax bargain. Alternatively, they may be induced to establish a nominal place of residence, a tax address."

Since the early 1980s, there has been a fairly widespread reduction among countries in the marginal tax rates levied on the incomes of individuals. Especially in the Anglo-Saxon countries, the reductions in *marginal* tax rates have been large.[18] In other countries, the reductions have been more modest but still significant. It is not clear whether this process has reduced effective tax differences among countries and has thus brought about some kind of spontaneous coordination. Revenue statistics related to tax collection from individual income taxes do not, however, reveal any trends. For the whole OECD area, the weighted average of total revenue from personal income taxes as a percentage of GDP was 11.4 percent in 1980 and 11.6 percent in 1991. The dispersion in the effective average tax rates across countries does not seem to have changed much either, and there is as yet no clear evidence that small countries have experienced greater revenue falls than large ones except for taxes on personal income.

The main policy conclusion that follows from the discussion in this chapter is that especially small countries should be careful in not taxing those with exceptional talent with too-heavy tax rates. This policy, however, is difficult to implement because it is difficult to make a distinction between normal labor and exceptional labor. The best that a country can do is to reduce the highest marginal tax rates, which are the ones more likely to affect those with high incomes. This policy is, of course, consistent with recent trends and with the views of many economists concerned about the efficiency implications of taxation. It just adds one more reason to do so. Deeper integration is likely to increase the mobility of the most able individuals and thus to increase the role of taxation. The more important taxation is in the process of the brain drain, the greater the pressure, especially on small countries, to reduce the level and the progressivity of taxes on labor income.

The above discussion has not identified areas in which tax harmonization, or even some form of tax coordination, should or will soon become necessary or even likely. Countries will continue to respond individually to the pressures on their most valuable people associated with deep integration and with differential tax rates. However, there is

18. They have been close to 40 percentage points in the United States, 20 percentage points in the United Kingdom, and about 15 percentage points in Canada.

an important issue that should perhaps be raised at this point. It is an issue that will acquire more prominence when the taxation of financial incomes is discussed. This is the issue of whether global income taxes can survive in a world undergoing a process of deep integration.

Musgrave starts chapter 8 of his classic work with the sentence, "Perhaps the most widely accepted principle of equity in taxation is that people in equal positions should be treated equally." After arguing that income is the "best index of equality," he writes:

> The concept of taxable income which has gained increasing acceptance among fiscal theorists is that of total accretion. Income is defined to equal consumption during a given period, plus increase in net worth. According to this concept, all accretions to wealth are included, in whatever form they are received or from whatever source they accrue. Factor earnings such as rents, interest, profits, and wages are included.[19]

In other words, all the incomes derived by an individual are combined in a global income and are taxed in the same way independently from their composition. This tax rate, of course, although not affected by the composition of income, is affected by its level. This global income taxation approach, originally promoted by Henry Simons and subsequently strongly supported by influential economists such as Richard Goode and Joseph Pechman, proved to be very influential.[20] Many countries have aimed at introducing a global income tax. However, the integration of the world economies can make the pursuit of this objective very costly when the international mobility of some tax bases is much greater than that of others. Deeper integration may force countries to reassess the policy of taxing global income and may induce them to introduce explicitly or implicitly a schedular approach to income taxation, so that for the more mobile bases, a country will compete with other countries by reducing the tax rates only on those incomes and not on all incomes.

There is some indication that this is already happening. For example, Sørensen has described how the Nordic countries have introduced a system of dual income taxation that combines progres-

---

19. Musgrave (1959, pp. 160, 165).
20. See Simons (1938); Simons (1950); Goode (1976); Pechman (1987).

sive taxation of labor and transfer incomes with a proportional tax on income from capital.[21]

Of course, it is also possible that increased coordination or even harmonization may result, so that countries will not have to change their approach to income taxation drastically. In any case there will be a tendency for high tax rates to come down even more than they have in recent years.

21. Sørensen (1994).

Chapter 5

Trade Liberalization and Indirect Taxation

*I*N recent years, trade liberalization has been proceeding at a relatively fast pace despite the continuing threat of protectionism and the difficulties that were encountered in pushing the Uruguay Round to a successful conclusion. Since 1946, there have been eight General Agreement on Tariffs and Trade (GATT) rounds on tariff reductions. According to figures reported by the International Monetary Fund (IMF), in the period 1985–92 world trade volume grew at a simple average rate of 5.1 percent a year while world output grew at a simple average rate of 2.6 percent.[1] Jacob Frenkel, Assaf Razin, and Efraim Sadka have reported that the average tariff rate in industrial countries fell from about 40 percent in 1950 to less than 5 percent in 1980 while the ratio of exports to the gross national product (GNP) rose from 7 to 17 percent.[2] This trend has continued or even accelerated since 1980. Thus at least with respect to the production and consumption of goods, the world economy has definitely become more integrated.

Foreign Trade Taxes

Many obstacles besides taxes still put breaks to the free movement of goods, and the importation of services is still discriminated against in many countries. Besides the obstacles imposed by various kinds of regulations (justified on health, environmental, cultural, and other

1. International Monetary Fund (1993, pp. 93, 113).
2. Frenkel, Razin, and Sadka (1991, p. 212).

grounds) and besides other subtle obstacles more difficult to identify but real all the same, trade is influenced by indirect taxes.[3] The most obvious tax influences are still those associated with foreign trade taxes—export and import taxes. These taxes have lost importance in industrial countries but remain important in developing countries, where they still generate, on the average, about one-third of their tax revenue.[4]

Until the early 1980s, export duties generated about 1 percent of the gross domestic product (GDP) of developing countries and almost 2 percent for low-income developing countries. They now generate an almost insignificant amount of revenue in both developing and developed countries. An export tax is conceptually equivalent to an ad valorem tax on the production of the taxed product and an ad valorem subsidy on the domestic consumption of that product. In other words, although it discourages domestic production, it encourages domestic consumption. It is thus an antitrade measure par excellence. The progressive elimination of export taxes is a change that has improved the allocation of world resources as well as the allocation of resources within the exporting countries.[5] At present, most economists would favor their elimination, and governments have seen the wisdom of eliminating them. In conclusion, a deeply integrating world would have no use for these taxes, and there is no need for a coordinated approach toward their elimination.

Import duties continue to be widely used in developing countries for both revenue reasons and for protecting domestic industries and inducing import substitution. Given the difficulties of imposing domestic taxes, imports provide to some countries a convenient tax handle for obtaining revenue. An import duty on a product X has the same effect of an equivalent ad valorem tax on the domestic consumption of that product and an equivalent ad valorem subsidy on the domestic production of that product. By raising the domestic price of the product, the tax discourages its consumption while it

3. One example is testing sights for imported products that are very far from the frontiers.

4. The OECD does not bother to classify them separately in its summary tables in the *Revenue Statistics.*

5. In the past, lots of apologists attempted to justify these taxes on various grounds for developing countries. In fact, it is easy to think of cases in which these taxes could be justified on *theoretical* grounds.

attracts resources to its inefficient production.[6] Infant industry arguments and other arguments based on externalities and other theoretical considerations have often been used to justify import duties. However, regardless of the validity of those arguments for specific conditions, most economists remain convinced that these taxes distort the allocation of resources not just for the whole world but especially for the countries that impose them. These arguments have begun to fall on receptive ears in many developing countries.

Import duties continue to be used mainly by developing countries, where they remain important for raising tax revenue. In industrial countries, they have lost importance but have not disappeared. As recently as 1913, they accounted for about 50 percent of U.S. federal tax revenue. They now generate insignificant amounts of revenue. Their justification as tools for the industrialization of countries has also lost some of its former attraction as models of development based on import substitution are no longer fashionable. Nominal rates have been coming down, but the replacement of quantitative restrictions with tariffs and the imposition of import duties on raw materials have left average revenue from this source broadly unchanged as shares of the GDPs of developing countries taken as a group.

There is now little debate that where the administrative possibility for a shift exists, these taxes should be replaced by domestic indirect taxes that interfere less with the allocation of resources and with the free movement of goods. Deep integration would require the complete elimination of both import and export taxes. There is much progress still to be made in this area. The success of the value-added tax (VAT) in many developing countries is partly due to the attempt to replace import duties with domestic indirect taxes. One can expect that this trend will continue and that at some future but not-too-distant date foreign trade taxes will come to play an inconsequential role in the movement of goods across countries. Import duties lead to frictions among countries, especially when large countries continue to use them after other countries have eliminated them.

---

6. Because of differential duties on final product and on inputs, effective protection levels are often much higher than nominal duties. Thus the nominal duties do not necessarily provide an idea of the degree of protection given to the protected activity.

General Sales Taxes

Domestic indirect taxes include general sales taxes and excises. General sales taxes come in many shapes and forms, but they can be broadly classified under three headings: traditional (cascading) turnover taxes, retail taxes, and VATs.

Turnover taxes were very popular around the world in years past, and they existed in many European countries until recent decades. (The United States is among the few countries that never had such a tax.) They continue to exist in developing countries but have disappeared in industrial countries.[7] In Europe, these taxes have been replaced by VATs. The same trend is taking place in developing countries and in economies in transition. The European Community replaced this tax with VATs to allow goods to move across countries without the interference of taxes. Turnover taxes tend to distort the free flow of goods and, consequently, the allocation of resources on a worldwide (and also domestic) basis. The degree of domestic distortion depends on the degree of integration of domestic enterprises. Enterprises integrated vertically have an advantage with this tax. In a deeply integrating world with complete free trade, there would be no place for this tax. Their elimination in Europe and other countries has been a positive step in improving the allocation of world resources. In Europe the replacement of turnover taxes with VATs represents one of the successful political attempts aimed at coordinating tax policies. The replacement in the rest of the world points to one of the successful spontaneous movements toward international tax coordination. Turnover taxes have been progressively and widely replaced by VATs.

The VAT, a newcomer to the field of taxation, has spread like wildfire during the past two decades. This has probably been the most important "technological" change in the field of taxation since the advent of the global income tax. All European countries as well as all American countries except the United States now adopt this tax.[8]

---

7. They also characterized the fiscal landscape of centrally planned economies although with some characteristics that reduced the cascading effect.

8. With the passage of this tax by the Venezuelan Parliament in September 1993, now all Latin American countries have a VAT. In November 1993, Switzerland voted to adopt a VAT. Puerto Rico is also studying the possibility of introducing a VAT.

Nine countries had this tax in the 1960s; twenty-eight in the 1970s; forty-eight in the 1980s; and about ninety countries by 1994.[9]

Trade liberalization and the introduction of the VAT are closely interrelated, although other features of this tax explain its growing popularity in the world. Despite some problems mentioned below, this tax has served the process of trade liberalization well. In fact, within the European Community the reason for the introduction of this tax was mainly its neutrality vis-à-vis trade across member countries and its administrability, especially when applied with the credit mechanism on the basis of the destination principle.[10] By 1973, the VAT had been introduced in all the nine countries then forming the European Community.[11]

The destination principle is consistent with the GATT guidelines, which require that the taxation of goods and services should take place in the country where they are consumed (destination principle) rather than where they are produced (origin principle). Therefore, the destination principle requires that taxes be imposed on the imports of goods and services and that exports should not be subject to taxation. In this way, domestic and foreign producers would compete fairly without tax distortions and without distorting the international allocation of resources. Equally important, each country is free to set the rates that it wants. To achieve the nontaxation of exports (for a tax imposed at several stages), it is necessary to compensate exporters for taxes paid at earlier stages of the production process by giving them tax rebates.

Theory has shown that the destination principle gives the same results as the origin principle if the tax is completely general in the sense that no activity is untaxed, if either the exchange rates or the price levels are completely flexible so that they come to reflect fully the effect on prices of the general sales tax, and if the stock of the

9. Tait (1988) and unpublished information compiled by Tait.

10. The credit mechanism implies that sellers can get credit against the tax they owe on their sales for the tax paid on inputs that were needed in connection with their sale. To get their credit, they must provide invoices of taxes actually paid. The destination principle states that when goods are exported, the exporters do not have to pay the VAT because the tax will be paid by the consumers of the countries where the goods are exported and consumed.

11. In an interesting example of technology transfer, from Europe the VAT found its way to Latin America and to French-speaking Africa.

factors of production is fixed.[12] The exchange rate or the price levels would adjust to reflect the differences in the rates of the general tax as had been recognized by Carl S. Shoup many years ago.[13] Thus the competitive situation of the country will not be changed. In this situation, either the destination principle or the origin principle would be consistent with a full national discretion over tax rates. Either principle would give the same outcome. Unfortunately, reality is different. Countries do not apply a single rate on *all* production or consumption, but they exempt or zero-rate some sectors[14]; the supply of capital and labor is not fixed but varies with the change in the tax level; prices are sticky, and exchange rates are not totally flexible or may even be fixed as they have been under the European Monetary System.[15] Furthermore, exchange rates are now increasingly influenced by capital movements.

A VAT applied with the destination principle is, in principle, an ideal tax with which to tax consumption in a world undergoing a process of integration. By allowing a credit on the purchase of capital goods, it allows governments to tax consumption alone. It also guarantees the independence of countries in determining the rates at which they wish to tax consumption. The allocation of world revenue from this tax is determined by two factors alone: the rate at which countries impose the VAT, and their consumption.[16] Because export prices do not reflect this tax, they are not distorted by attempts at manipulating trade. And because imports are taxed in the same way as domestically produced goods, they are not discriminated against. In a deeply integrating world but where national frontiers still exist, a VAT applied on the basis of the destination principle seems to have a lot going for it.

As is often the case, the practice and the *reality* can be somewhat different from the theory. A problem comes with the existence of

12. See Smith (1993).

13. See Shoup (1954).

14. The difference between exemption and zero rating is that exemption does not compensate a seller for taxes paid and incorporated at earlier stages. It only exempts the value added by the seller. Zero rating is supposed to remove the taxes incorporated at all stages.

15. See Tait (1993).

16. I ignore here differences in the efficiency of the tax administrations.

exemptions given to particular sectors. These may reflect administrative decisions that recognize the difficulties of taxing certain sectors (subsistence farming and small producers) or of identifying the value added produced by other sectors (financial institutions). These sectors do not pay taxes on their sales but also do not receive rebates for the taxes paid on their inputs. Therefore, the price of their sales contains a tax element that depends on the ratio of their own value added (that is, tax free) in the total value added and on the tax rates on the inputs. Because this ratio varies from sector to sector and even from producer to producer, there is clearly some tax-generated distortion in the final prices. The smaller the value added by (exempt) sellers and the higher the tax rates on the inputs for which the final sellers do not get a credit for the tax paid, the more disadvantaged these final sellers will be. If they are also exporters, they will be at a competitive disadvantage. Zero rating of these sectors (rather than exempting them) would reduce or eliminate this problem but would create other difficulties, mainly of an administrative nature.

A second problem comes from the need to have border controls when a VAT is levied on the basis of the destination principle using the credit mechanism. These border controls permit exporters to claim a rebate for the taxes paid on the exported goods. To get the rebate from the government for these taxes, the exporter needs to present the invoices that show the taxes paid and needs to give proof that the goods are exported. Border controls may impose substantial compliance costs on exporters, which may, in fact, reduce or even neutralize the beneficial effect of the VAT on trade. (See the long lines of trucks often waiting for hours or even days to cross the French-Italian frontiers of the Alps.) Therefore, deeply integrated areas such as the American states or deeply integrating areas such as the European Union would not want to have border controls.

These two problems reduce somewhat the attractiveness of the VAT as an ideal tax in a deeply integrating world. In such a world, taxes should not distort the prices that determine international trade but also should not impose high compliance costs.

At this point, it may be worthwhile to refer back to the example of the American federation and ask the question of whether *retail sales taxes,* which by definition reflect the destination principle because they are only collected from final consumers, could not provide an attractive alternative to the VAT. As Alan A. Tait stated, "Many of us still have a sentimental affection for more simple retail sales taxes (RST) that could achieve similar results." The answer to this question is simple. Provided that the rates at which the RST is imposed are low and are not too different between (especially neighboring) countries, the RST is a good alternative to the VAT. Given these conditions, the RST could thus be a desirable tax in a deeply integrating world. According to Tait, "The VAT is the only common sales tax in a customs union, other than a retail sales tax, that fulfills the obligations for tax neutrality on traded goods and services under the General Agreement on Tariffs and Trade."[17] However, other considerations may change this conclusion. In many industrial countries and even in some developing countries (Argentina, Brazil, Chile) that use the VAT, this tax raises revenue between 5 and more than 10 percent of the GDP (table 5-1). This level of revenue productivity typically requires tax rates of the order of 15 to 25 percent. In fact, the average unweighted revenue productivity from the VAT in industrial countries is 7.16 percent of the GDP collected, with an average rate of 17.2 percent.[18] The average revenue productivity per unit of standard rate is 0.43 percent of the GDP.

In the United States, in 1991, the total share in the GDP of retail sales taxes collected by states and localities was 2.25 percent. This revenue was collected with rates that ranged from 0 percent in the five states that did not use these taxes to 7.5 percent in Connecticut.[19] In other words, the industrial countries that used the VAT in 1991 raised more than three times more revenue from general sales taxes (as shares of the GDP) than the United States. To raise this higher revenue, these countries had to impose rates that were at least three times as high as in the American states. The key question then is whether countries could still retain the flexibility to raise large amounts of tax revenue from general sales taxes if they relied on the RST rather than on VATs.

An important empirical observation is that countries that have relied on RSTs "tend to charge around 4–6 percent of the tax-exclu-

---

17. Tait (1988, pp. 7, 20–21).

18. Actually the 17.2 percent refers to the *standard* rate that generates an overwhelming share of revenue. However, several countries have reduced or high rates as well. It is thus difficult to measure the average rate precisely.

19. Based on Advisory Commission on Intergovernmental Relations (1993a, pp. 103–13; 1993b, p. 79).

Table 5-1. *Value-Added Taxes in Industrial Countries, 1991*

Percent

Country	Standard rate (%) (1)	VAT revenue as share of GDP (%) (2)	VAT revenue per unit rate (%) (2) ÷ (1) = (3)
Denmark	25	8.89	0.36
Sweden	25	8.87	0.35
Iceland	24	10.14	0.42
Finland	22	8.46	0.38
Ireland	21	7.44	0.35
Austria	20	8.54	0.43
Norway	20	8.18	0.41
Belgium	19	7.20	0.38
Italy	19	5.68	0.30
France	18	7.73	0.43
Greece	18	9.39	0.52
Netherlands	17.5	7.33	0.42
United Kingdom	17.5	6.65	0.38
Portugal	16	6.17	0.39
Germany	15	6.42	0.43
Luxembourg	15	9.41	0.63
Spain	15	5.43	0.36
New Zealand	12.5	8.55	0.68
Turkey	12	5.91	0.49
Canada	7	2.72	0.39
Japan	3	1.37	0.46
Average	17.2	7.17	0.43

Source: Estimated by the author on the basis of information obtained from OECD (1991a); rates assembled by Alan Tait from the tax laws for individual countries.

sive value of goods, . . . whereas standard VAT rates tend to vary between 14 and 25 percent."[20] Tait has reported that "only Iceland, Norway, South Africa, Sweden, and Zimbabwe have operated retail sales taxes at rates over 10 percent."[21] By now, all these countries except Zimbabwe have replaced the RST with the VAT. Nobody has accused the RST of being a "money machine" in the way people have referred to the VAT. The general view among experts, a view obviously shared by most governments, is that 10 percent may well be the

20. Messere (1993, p. 386).
21. Tait (1988, p. 18).

maximum rate feasible under an RST. A few comments are perhaps necessary to explain the reasons for this conclusion.[22]

In principle, the tax base for the RST and the VAT could be the same (consumption), so that applying a similar rate would provide similar revenue.[23] The RST is collected at one single point when the goods are sold to consumers. Up to that point, on sales from producers to other producers or from producers to wholesalers or from wholesalers to retailers, the tax is suspended. Thus the government receives no revenue until a retailer sells to a consumer. If a retailer evades the tax, the government loses the full tax liability on that sale. In many countries, there are many retailers and there is no paper trace that allows the tax administration to control them. By comparison, the VAT is due on the value added generated in each transaction, and to get a credit for the tax paid on their inputs (so that only their value added is taxed), sellers must keep invoices that must be made available to the government in case of an audit. Although tax evasion occurs with both taxes under normal administrative circumstances, it is more controllable with a VAT, and thus it is likely to be more limited, especially at high rates. If a retailer evades paying the VAT on its sales, the revenue loss will be limited to the liability connected with the value added at that stage because the tax would have been already paid in previous stages. These considerations have led Ken Messere to conclude that the VAT offers "considerable advantages" as regards robustness against tax evasion.[24] Again quoting Alan Tait, "At 5 percent, the incentive to evade [the retail sales] tax is probably not worth the penalties of prosecution; at 10 percent, evasion is more attractive, and at 15–20 percent, becomes extremely tempting."[25]

To collect from the RSTs the level of revenue currently collected from the VAT would require tax rates so high that they would create major problems of evasion. The inevitable conclusion is that if the current revenue levels continue to be necessary to sustain public expenditure without major macroeconomic imbalances, deep integra-

22. A very good discussion of the similarities and differences between the RST and the VAT is provided by Messere (1993, pp. 379–93). This source should be consulted for more details. See also the discussion in Tait (1988, chapter 1).

23. Attempts at measuring empirically the tax bases of these two taxes have not been very successful. However, they indicate that the tax base for the RST tends to be somewhat smaller than for the VAT. See Messere (1993, p. 386).

24. Messere (1993, p. 389).

25. Tait (1988, p. 18).

tion will induce or force countries that require high revenue to rely on the use of the VAT.[26] The alternative of the RST does not appear to be a practical one under the circumstances, although some countries with lower revenue needs could continue using the RST.

Having discussed the possibility that, as within the American states, the RST might provide an alternative to the VAT and having concluded that the RST is not a viable alternative under current revenue needs, we must go back to the second problem with VATs using the destination principle, namely, the need for border controls.

Given that border controls bring inefficiencies by imposing high compliance costs, VATs imposed with the destination principle may be assumed to be inconsistent with a process of deep integration that forces the removal of national frontiers. In fact, this has been the basic conclusion reached by the European Community (EC; now the European Union), which, as a consequence, has progressively shown a predilection for a system that would dispense with border controls. In 1987, the EC Commission proposed a VAT system based on the origin principle, which, for exports, would require that the taxes be paid in the country where the goods are produced rather than in those where they are consumed. These taxes would thus be reflected in export prices. However, in such a system differences in the VAT rates would distort export prices and thus trade, leading the Commission to propose that VAT rates be harmonized among the member countries. In the absence of harmonized rates and with the origin principle, apart from the distortions in trading patterns that would inevitably occur, consumers would have an interest in shopping in countries where the rates were lowest, especially if the differences in rates were large and the distances to be traveled were small. This concern is heightened by the fact that 40 million Europeans live within twenty-five kilometers of the borders of their countries.

One could argue, as, in fact, it has been argued especially by the British government, that with the origin principle the differences in rates would be eliminated spontaneously by competitive forces. In other words, the countries imposing the highest rates would be free to

26. The IMF (1993, pp. 48–62) has called attention to the deteriorating fiscal situation in most industrial countries. Debt-to-GDP ratios are increasing in most of them, and fiscal deficits are high even when corrected for the effect of the recession. Conservative writers could argue that higher tax revenues do not necessarily reduce the size of the fiscal deficit. They could thus view the greater productivity of the VAT as a negative feature.

lower them, and the rate differences would be reduced to levels consistent with transaction costs associated with shopping outside of one's own jurisdiction. The net result of this process would be to force the high-rate countries to lower them and consequently accept the revenue losses associated with this reduction. Putting it more bluntly, the social preferences of the more conservative governments would be imposed on the less conservative ones.

However, some of these costs would exist also with a process of forced harmonization because countries would lose their freedom to impose the rates they wished and they would lose an important instrument of stabilization policy—that is, the ability to change the VAT rates to bring about desired changes in tax revenue. Both of these losses in the freedom of action of the countries imply efficiency or political costs that some countries are unwilling to bear. Another important consideration is that the revenues that the countries derive from their VATs would no longer be related to the size of their consumption but instead to the size of their taxable production. Those who sell more than they consume would gain in terms of tax revenue. Net exporters would gain; net importers would lose. To deal with this difficulty, the Commission proposed a clearinghouse that would reallocate revenue on the basis of the VAT declarations presented by the enterprises.

Negative reactions to this proposed scheme of harmonization of tax rates and of origin principle have, for the time being, led to an interim solution whereby border controls would be abolished among the EC countries. The destination principle would be maintained; however, the tax would be applied when the product is sold in the country of destination rather than at the frontier, when it is imported.[27] Also, the border controls would be replaced by administrative controls based on the auditing and the matching of the VAT declarations presented by enterprises. This system would presumably allow the member countries of the European Union to eliminate fiscal frontiers among themselves while retaining the freedom to use different tax rates. However, to reduce distortions that might increase in the absence of tax frontiers, the member states agreed to a package aimed at increasing the harmonization of the rates.

27. This aspect is supposed to give appreciable advantages, in terms of liquidity, to the importers because they no longer need to anticipate the tax payment to the time when they import the goods, which is ahead of the time when the goods are sold.

Table 5-2. *VAT Rates Applicable in the Member States of the European Union on May 1, 1993*
Percent

Country	Reduced rate	Standard rate	Increased rate
Belgium	1–6–12	19.5	...
Denmark	0	25	...
France	2.1–5.5	18.6	...
Germany	7	15	...
Greece	4–8	18	...
Ireland	2.5–12.5	21	...
Italy	4–9–12	19	...
Luxembourg	3–6–12	15	...
Netherlands	6	17.5	...
Portugal	5	16	30[a]
Spain	3–6	15	...
United Kingdom	0	17.5	...

Source: Author's estimates based on unpublished information from the European Union.
a. The application of the increased rate by Portugal is contrary to current European Union rules.

The new system went into effect on January 1, 1993, when border controls between the countries of the European Union were removed.[28] The removal of these controls eliminated the mechanism of border tax adjustments, which had permitted the traditional application of the destination principle. As an interim system (until a definitive VAT system based on the origin principle comes into effect, perhaps by 1997 but most likely later), the destination principle has been maintained by substituting inland controls for border controls. Thus a kind of postponed accounting system was introduced by which an import VAT is self-imposed by the first taxable entity in the importing country, and export rebates are provided on the basis of documentary evidence that the goods have been actually sold abroad.

A step toward the harmonization of VAT rates was taken when in June 1991 the member states of the then EC agreed that the VATs would have a standard rate of at least 15 percent and, at most, two reduced rates of at least 5 percent for a list of seventeen products. They also agreed to eliminate the increased rates, those above the standard rate. The 15 percent rate is equivalent to the lowest standard rate now in use in Germany, Luxembourg, and Spain (table 5-2).

28. The assistance of Edward Gardner in preparing this description of recent changes in Europe is much appreciated.

In 1993, there were still large differences in the EC rates—10 percentage points between Denmark (with 25 percent) and Germany, Luxembourg, and Spain. These differences can create problems by inducing individuals to cross frontiers to reduce their tax payments. These problems are significant when the rate differences are large, the countries are contiguous, and the purchases concern expensive items.

An early assessment of the new regime has been "broadly positive." As far as the heavy administrative burdens, "the key elements of the new system, such as communication between traders of VAT identification numbers and conservation of the proof of transport outside the Member States of departure, have been easily adopted."[29] Tax evasion and tax fraud have been minimized by strengthened administrative effort in each administration and by an intense effort aimed at increasing the exchange of information among tax administrations. VAT identification numbers, preceded by the country code, have been assigned to traders. Exporters have been required to report the VAT identification number of their foreign customers to claim rebates for their exports. This information is made available to the tax authorities of the importing countries.[30] Since November 1992, "the VAT Information Exchange System (VIES) has enabled traders to obtain confirmation of their customers' VAT identification numbers."[31] There is no clear-cut evidence to indicate that tax evasion has increased. However, the current recession and its effect on revenue makes it difficult to isolate the effect of the new tax regime from the effect of the recession. Falls in VAT revenues have generally been attributed to the effects of the recession. However, tax evasion is often a dynamic process associated with learning by doing. It is a process that also has externalities in the sense that once a taxpayer learns a new way of beating the system, other taxpayers come to learn it and to follow it. With the passing of time, taxpayers will probe the new system for its weaknesses. It is too early to pass judgment on the new regime.

29. See the communication by Christianne Scrivener, the European Union tax commissioner, on "Six Months' Operation of the New Indirect Tax Regime: A Broadly Positive Initial Assessment" (Luxembourg, October 25, 1993). This assessment has been shared by more detached observers. For example, Albert J. Rädler has concluded that "in general, it can be said that the transition went more smoothly [for the VAT] than anticipated." See Rädler (1993).

30. Because individuals do not have these VAT identification numbers, sales to them create additional administrative burdens.

31. Scrivener, "Six Months' Operation," p. 4.

As table 5-2 shows, there are still large tax rate differentials among countries. This fact, together with the recently acquired freedom on the part of individuals to engage in cross-border shopping without restrictions or limitations, raises the obvious question about the extent to which trade distortions could become larger. The cross-border shopping by individuals is seen as unavoidable and so far is not considered a major issue. However, the reduced rates imposed by many countries are seen as causing some distortions in competitiveness. Also, distance sales made through catalogue, telephone, or computer are increasing in importance and may lead to significant trade distortions and to shifting of VAT revenue as long as the tax rate differentials remain large.

The Commission would like to replace the current "temporary" regime by a definitive regime based on the "origin" principle. Such a regime, which the Commission would like to bring into effect by 1997, would no longer allow VAT rebates on exported products. Purchases would be taxed on the bases of the tax rates of the countries in which they take place (the country of origin). However, importers would be able to take a credit for the tax paid on their purchases against their own tax liabilities on their sales in their own countries. As long as information flows freely and efficiently between the tax administrations of the two countries, the tax chain between producer and consumer, that is, the main strength of the VAT, would be recreated. However, in an international setting such an efficient flow of information cannot be taken for granted. One problem with this proposed system is that it would redistribute VAT revenue from countries that are net importers (within the European Union) and that have lower VAT rates toward countries that are net exporters (within the European Union) and that have higher tax rates. The Commission has proposed that a "clearinghouse" redistribute revenue on the basis of the allocation that would result from the application of the destination principle, but doubts persist as to how this system would work. Harmonization of rates would alleviate but not eliminate the problem.

Excise Taxes

Excise taxes are taxes levied on the sale of particular goods and services. They can be collected at the retail level when consumers buy the taxed commodity, or they can be collected at the manufacturing stage where the commodities are produced. The basic characteristics of these taxes are that they fall on specific products rather than on general consumption and that they do not distinguish in a legal sense between domestically produced and imported products. Thus a tax imposed only on the import of a given commodity and not on the same commodity produced domestically is an import duty and not an excise tax.

Excise taxes are imposed for various reasons: to raise revenue; to tax some individuals for benefits they may receive from activities associated with the consumption of the taxed commodity, as is the case for gasoline and the free use of roads; to discourage the use of some commodity that is damaging to health, as with cigarettes; to penalize the users of some commodities for negative externalities they may impose on society, as with alcoholic beverages; or to attempt to give some progressivity to the tax system by taxing luxury products.

Because these taxes are imposed on particular products and not on others, they are, by their very nature, distortive. However, especially when they are imposed for reasons associated with use benefits, health issues, and negative externalities, the distortions created by the taxes are not necessarily welfare-reducing. However, when they are imposed for reasons associated with raising revenues and taxing luxury products, they generally impose distortions that tend to be welfare-reducing. The higher the tax rate and the higher the elasticity of the demand for the taxed good, the greater will be the welfare cost associated with the tax. The reason is that a high tax rate imposed on a price-elastic commodity can change the pattern of consumption away from the desired pattern, which is the one that maximizes welfare. This distortion is costly, in welfare terms.

In open economies other issues arise in connection with these taxes. In general, excise taxes are imposed on imports with the same rates and the same conditions as imposed on the domestic production of the taxed commodity. Furthermore, exports are not subjected to these taxes but are taxed (at destination) in the country where the exported commodities are consumed. Openness may give some countries the possibility to use these taxes to exploit international movements of goods and people to get some advantages. Alternatively, openness may reduce a country's degree of freedom in connection with the use of these taxes. In this chapter, some of these issues are explored to determine the implications of deepening integration for the freedom of particular countries to impose the excise taxes they choose and the effect of these taxes on resource allocation.

When foreign trade taxes were discussed, it was concluded that in an integrating world there should be no place for import duties because they interfere with free trade and with an optimal world, and even country, allocation of resources. Unfortunately, excise taxes have been and continue to be used as proxies for import duties. For example, an excise tax on bananas imposed by European or North American countries would be an example of such a misuse of import duties. Such an excise would have the objective of protecting the production of fruits that grow in these countries and that compete against bananas. It is not surprising to find that excise taxes on wine are very high in northern European countries and low in wine-producing southern European countries. It is equally not surprising to find that the reverse is true for beer, whiskey, gin, and similar alcoholic beverages. Each of these groups of countries is using excise taxes as protective devises for some of their domestic production.

A look back at the reasons for imposing the excises listed above points to problems that may arise, especially when countries are contiguous, the goods taxed have high value and low weight, and the frontiers are open and near. Take the case of cigarettes or alcoholic beverages. Suppose that countries A and B are neighbors. Suppose also that the frontiers are open and the distances short.[32] Suppose also that country A wishes to impose high taxes on cigarettes and alcohol for health and externalities reasons. Country B is less concerned about the health effects of cigarettes and the externalities effects of alcohol. It may then be to country B's advantage to impose excise taxes on cigarettes and alcoholic beverages that are significantly lower than in A. In fact, if country B has information on the price elasticity of demand for these products by the citizens of country A and has information about transportation costs, it can calculate optimal tax rates that would maximize its revenue by attracting the maximum amount of purchases from the citizens of country A. This would be a

32. Cross-border shopping will depend on travel costs. These include explicit costs (such as gasoline or train tickets) and time costs. For empirical evidence of cross-border shopping between Northern Ireland and the Irish Republic, see FitzGerald and others (1988).

classic case of tax competition, whereby country B would attempt to export some of its tax collection. In this case, if country A retaliates by cutting the rates of its excises, it could find itself with a level of consumption of cigarettes and alcohol that it considers excessive.

As was seen in the discussion of the cigarette taxes in the American states, tax exporting is not a theoretical possibility but one that will need to be reckoned with in an integrating world. As transportation becomes easier and cheaper and frontiers become more open, one can expect that attempts at tax exporting will increase. These attempts may worsen the allocation of resources or, at times, even improve it. But they will reduce the freedom of the taxing countries to impose excise taxes at levels they wish. For example, a country that wanted to raise tax revenue, and conceivably the equity of its tax system, by taxing expensive jewelry with high excise taxes would not be able to do so or would be disappointed in the revenue it got if its residents could easily shop in other countries with lower tax rates.[33]

High tax rates on some easy-to-carry products such as cameras, videos, and watches were possible in the past because borders were relatively closed, people did not travel much, and foreign purchases were not easy. However, as the flow of information increases, people travel more, and frontiers become more open, it will become progressively more difficult to keep these taxes high. Competition will push these taxes progressively down unless attempts are made at some harmonization of rates at least in neighboring countries. The EC attempted to alleviate this problem by asking member countries to adopt minimum rates for the excises that apply on tobacco products, mineral oils, and alcoholic beverages. Furthermore, future changes would be toward common target rates. An original attempt to harmonize the rates was resisted by some countries on the basis of revenue losses that would accompany these changes.[34]

For the world at large, excise tax rates still remain widely divergent, and it is obvious that some countries have been benefiting by attracting foreign buyers to them by holding down the excise rates for particularly sensitive products. One can only guess that the trend

33. Of course, given the probably high elasticity of the demand for expensive jewelry, an excise on this commodity would have substantial welfare costs. Thus one can argue that in this case tax competition could be welfare-enhancing.

34. For a very good discussion of the efficiency gain from indirect tax harmonization, see Keen (1993).

might be some spontaneous leveling of rate differences because there is at the moment no mechanism and no international institution that would attempt to bring a more coordinated or political harmonization process. However, leveling through competition is likely to be accompanied by a general reduction in the tax rates with inevitable revenue consequences.

One type of excise that has implications that go well beyond the annoyance of cross-border shopping and that deserves much more attention than it has received because of its potential for large reallocation if not misallocation of resources on a worldwide basis is the excise on petroleum products.

The taxation of petroleum among countries presents enormous differences, which undoubtedly induce different levels and patterns of consumption and which may induce major reallocation of resources on a world basis. These tax differences are important for all kinds of energy products but become truly large with respect to gasoline. Table 5-3 shows the very large variation in the price of gasoline in the first quarter of 1993 among the Organization for Economic Cooperation and Development (OECD) countries. These prices vary from a low of $0.294 a liter in the United States to a maximum of $1.206 a liter for Norway, where the price of gasoline was 4.10 times larger than in the United States. The table shows that the price differences were largely the result of the excise taxes imposed by the various countries. The shares of these taxes in the prices of gasoline in the OECD countries varied from a low of 29.6 percent in the United States to a maximum of almost 78 percent in France.

If these excises reflected negative externalities imposed by gasoline use in different countries, they could be assumed to be consistent with an efficient allocation of resources across countries, but this is not the case. The high taxes basically reflect high needs of revenue and greater willingness on the part of the governments of some countries to impose these high taxes and for the citizens to tolerate them. In the United States, citizens are much more opposed to these taxes than are those of most of the European countries.[35]

35. Within the United States the state gasoline taxes ranged from a low of 8 cents a gallon in Alaska and New York to a high of 26 cents a gallon in Connecticut and Rhode Island. These rates exclude county and local taxes. See Advisory Commission on Intergovernmental Relations (1993a, p. 116).

Table 5-3. *Gasoline Prices and Gasoline Taxes in OECD Countries, First Quarter, 1993*

Country	Price (US$ per liter)	Gasoline taxes (% of price)
France	0.946	77.9
Greece	0.909	75.3
Sweden	1.067	74.8
Italy	1.014	74.3
Portugal	0.980	73.9
Germany	0.924	73.8
Netherlands	1.072	72.9
Norway	1.206	72.0
Belgium	0.977	71.6
Finland	0.929	71.3
Spain	0.854	68.8
United Kingdom	0.765	68.3
Switzerland	0.709	67.7
Ireland[a]	1.001	66.6
Denmark	0.931	66.1
Luxembourg	0.759	65.7
Austria	0.922	65.0
Canada	0.432	47.6
Australia	0.458	47.0
Japan	1.025	46.0
New Zealand	0.535	45.8
United States	0.294	29.6

Source: International Energy Agency (1993, pp. 284, 293).
a. 1992.

This different taxation of petroleum products—and similar conclusions apply to other forms of energy—and especially the very low level of taxes in the United States, brings with it some important consequences. Only a few are mentioned here; a complete analysis of this issue would require a specialized study.

First, the very high petroleum taxes imposed in other countries, and especially in Europe and Japan, reduce the level of consumption in those countries. Depending on the elasticity of demand for this product, consumption must be reduced marginally or substantially. For sure, over the longer run the elasticity and thus the reduction in consumption must be much higher than in the short run. As a consequence of the low taxes in the United States that is likely to increase demand in that large country, the international price of petroleum, net of taxes, must be kept at levels somewhat higher than would be the case if the United States imposed taxes similar to those imposed in Europe and Japan. If the United States imposed these tax levels, total world demand would fall. Alternatively, if Europe and Japan lowered their taxes to the American level, the net-of-tax world price of petroleum would rise because aggregate world demand would rise.

The high petroleum taxes in Europe and Japan can be seen as partly a tax on petroleum producers, because these receive lower prices for their petroleum than they would get in the absence of these high taxes, and partly as a subsidy to the consumers of those countries, and especially those in the United States, that benefit from the lower prices brought about by the lower world consumption. How these burdens and subsidies are distributed depends on the elasticities of supply and demand for petroleum as well as for other sources of energy. However these burdens and subsidies are shared, they must imply major reallocation if not misallocation of resources on a world scale.

Oil-exporting countries have shown increasing awareness of these issues and increasing annoyance toward the countries that impose high excise taxes on gasoline consumption. They have called for the reduction or even the removal of these taxes so that, they believe, they can get their fair compensation for their petroleum exports. This is an issue that is likely to become hot in future years, as it was when OPEC was created.

Because of the low cost of petroleum and energy in general, American consumers are likely to consume more of this product than their European or Japanese counterparts. More speculatively, it is also likely that a larger proportion of the savings of American families is spent on durable goods that require significant energy use, including housing and large cars, than in other countries. In fact, a study has shown that American families invest a larger share of their savings in durable goods than families of other industrial countries even when income differentials are taken into account.[36] This difference might be due to the cost of energy.

A realistic hypothesis could be that the total cost, discounted to the present, of buying and using, during their useful life, durable con-

36. Lipsey and Kravis (1987).

sumer goods (cars, refrigerators, air conditioners, houses) is highly sensitive to the cost of energy and to the real rate of interest. This total cost is made up of the initial purchase cost of the durable good and the running costs over the life of the asset. These running costs are largely the interest payments, implicit or explicit, and the price of energy.[37] If, because of the integration of financial markets, real interest rates tend to converge and, because of free trade, the cost of tradable durables also tends to converge, then the relative cost of energy to the consumers of different countries would be the main factor in determining the discounted cost of using these assets.[38] If the low price of energy and the deductibility of nominal interest payments combine to reduce the cost of durable goods sharply, a larger proportion of family income could go into these goods, thus reducing the savings of families and the savings available for other uses.

The above discussion points to the advantages of having similar taxes on energy. Without similar tax treatment of energy use, substantial international reallocation of resources takes place. Of course, similar taxes is not understood to mean identical taxes because differences based on externalities could, for example, justify differential carbon taxes across countries. Externalities based on traffic congestion could do the same.

This discussion has called attention to the need for less differentiation in the taxation of petroleum products and other energy products, but it has not indicated what the optimal price of energy should be. Presumably, this price would depend on the long-run costs of producing energy and on the environmental and other costs that energy consumption imposes on the nations and on the world. The discussion has focused on the taxation of petroleum to consumers. To the extent that the prices to producers also differ substantially, there would be not just efficiency costs in consumption but also efficiency costs in production. These latter costs may also influence the allocation of capital in the world.

An argument could be made that, in the absence of physical externalities, there is no reason why each country could not choose the tax regime that it wants. If Italians want to pay $4.00 a gallon of

37. Of course, one would also take into account repair costs and depreciation costs and, for houses and cars, property and registration or license taxes.

38. Actually, another important tax consideration would be whether interest payments could be deducted. This issue is discussed subsequently.

gasoline, while the Venezuelans want to pay $0.15 a gallon, why is this an international concern? The point is that—quite apart from traditional economic externalities, which cannot be ignored—there are other kinds of spillovers that in a progressively integrating world become important. For example, the low saving rate of the United States is widely perceived as having important international implications because it raises the world real rate of interest. Similarly, seen through European eyes, the heavy use of petroleum by the United States raises the world price of petroleum and thus increases other countries' cost for it. Seen through oil producers' eyes, European and Japanese high taxation of petroleum reduces earnings from oil production. These international ramifications are attracting progressively more attention and generating an increasing level of friction. This friction can be prevented by coordination of policies among countries.

Chapter 6

Economic Integration and Capital Taxation

*I*N no other area of taxation can the effect of deepening economic integration be as unsettling or as important as in the taxation of capital. Although for other tax bases economic integration can create significant distortions and difficulties, their effect is to damage and not destroy the existing system. For capital taxation, however, when the process of economic integration is deep, the outcome can be more drastic. Deep integration can shake the very foundations on which capital taxation has been built. It can create fault lines in those foundations that can become wide enough to bring down, at least in theory, the whole structure. This is the reason why an increasing number of tax experts has been making dire predictions about the future of capital taxation.

For example, Roger H. Gordon has asked, "Can capital income taxes survive in open economies?"[1] In the same spirit, Jack M. Mintz asked, "Is there a future for capital income taxation?"[2] For Guttorm Schjelderup, "the fear is that capital mobility may lead to capital flight from high to low tax countries in such large amounts that it deprives a nation of its tax base and, as a consequence, its welfare system."[3] Similar fears have been expressed by other authors, including Frenkel, Razin, and Sadka.[4] These fears are related to the taxation of capital in all countries but acquire special urgency in small countries. Small countries may find it particularly difficult to maintain high tax

1. Gordon (1990).
2. Mintz (1992).
3. Schjelderup (1993, p. 377).
4. Frenkel, Razin, and Sadka (1991, p. 213).

rates on capital income, and some of them may be tempted to become "tax havens" for foreign capital, thus making it more difficult for other countries to maintain their tax rates.[5] As Razin and Sadka have put it, "No capital income tax, whatsoever, can be efficiently imposed by a small open economy if capital flight to the rest of the world cannot be effectively stopped."[6] Of course, for capital to move out of a given country the net-of-tax rate of return in the rest of the world must be lower than that in the country. The idea that especially small countries will be exposed to the effects of deep integration on capital taxation is a recurrent theme in the literature on international taxation.

These fears about the future of capital taxation are now shared by a sizable number of tax experts. However, as is seen later, there has still not been any specific and coordinated policy response to this challenge, and there is still limited evidence that revenue from taxes on capital income has fallen in the world. Capital taxation is an area in which neither coordination nor harmonization has taken place even within the European Union. In the European Union, the Commission responsible for taxation has been trying, so far without much success, to convince the member countries to make changes aimed at harmonizing their systems of capital taxation or at least at making them more compatible with one another.

The reason for this lack of action on the part of the national authorities may owe more to the uncertainty and disagreement among experts and policymakers on what to do than to political inertia, although the latter undoubtedly has played a role. As a European tax expert has put it, "In the disarray of this 'fin de siècle,' tax policymakers turn for guidance to the tax theorists, but find that little thought has been given to the shape and form of a comprehensive tax system that is up to the challenge of the new regional and global scene."[7] So far, the results from theoretical analysis have been useful for identifying problems but not for suggesting solutions. Such solutions would have to take into account different political biases, different country sizes, different needs for tax revenue, different possibilities of exploiting tax competition to derive particular advantages,

5. See, among others, Kanbur and Keen (1993); Razin and Sadka (1991).

6. Razin and Sadka (1991, p. 15).

7. See Hinnekens (1992, p. 157). A sketch of a strategy for reform has been suggested by Giovannini (1990).

different legal systems, and different tax structures. These theoretical studies tell us what problems will develop as deep integration intensifies and the fault lines in the existing structure widen, but they do not suggest practical and realistic solutions for dealing with these developing problems. In any case, a first best solution is unlikely to be achievable as long as the tax systems remain the exclusive responsibility of particular countries and these countries continue to have conflicting objectives.

For the foreseeable future, there seems to be no possibility of developing a tax system that transcends the countries' responsibilities. Even within the European Union, there has been so far no talk of a European tax administration and a truly European system. The assumption continues to be that each member country will continue to have its own tax structure and tax administration and that, somehow, such an alternative with some policy and administrative adjustments will be viable. As Luc Hinnekens has put it, "The territoriality principle thus becomes the soft underbelly of the tax system. But there is no good substitute for it. . . . It is . . . illusory and disastrous for tax policy makers and tax theorists to believe that tax jurisdiction can be based on other than tax territory principles."[8]

The taxation of capital income, especially in its international dimensions, is extremely complex. Few if any individuals understand all its rules and ramifications, and hundreds of books and articles by economists, lawyers, and accountants have been written. It would thus be futile for this study to attempt to outline or summarize that literature or to give a comprehensive account of it. Rather, the objective here is to try to focus on the main elements in the taxation of capital that are subject to increasing pressures caused by the intensifying process of economic integration—in other words, the widening fault lines.

To understand why many economists and tax experts are wondering whether the existing structure of capital income taxation will survive the process of deepening integration, it may be helpful to focus briefly on the traditional architecture of capital taxation, an architecture that, it should be remembered, was created mostly when, for various reasons (wars, depression), the economies of the industrial

8. Hinnekens (1992, p. 156). The "territory principle" means the country responsibility for taxation in its own territory. Thus countries will continue to apply taxes on their territory even when the lines that divide territories may become legally invisible.

countries were relatively closed and information flowed slowly and was limited and thus capital hardly moved across countries. That architecture is still largely intact despite the fact that the countries' economies are now much more open and integrated and that capital movements have become enormous.

The first essential element is the national, or in some cases subnational, character of the taxes on capital. These taxes are levied by countries or by subnational jurisdictions such as the states in the United States.[9] This implies or assumes a special relationship between the taxing country and the subjects taxed, be these individuals or legal entities. The working assumption is that these subjects are for the most part *citizens* of the country or *national* enterprises. This relationship is based on the principle of territoriality that gives the government of a given geographic area the right to tax the subjects that reside in that area and the activities that take place in it to raise revenue to finance governmental objectives such as income redistribution and spending for public goods.

Almost all taxes are justified to some extent on the basis of the principle of benefit received taxation. Even when the principle advocated is ability to pay (that presumably helps the government to promote a better distribution of income), it can be argued, and, in fact, it has been argued by some economists, that taxation based on ability to pay principle will make the country a better place to live and will thus benefit everyone living in it. This implicit element of benefit taxation always increases the legitimacy of the taxing actions of the government. It is unlikely that taxation based purely on and justified by ability to pay without any connection to benefits would ever survive in a democratic country.

The second essential element is the traditional, or historical, assumption that much of the income of the taxpayers originates from within the jurisdiction and thus benefits from the expenditure by the government. At the time when the architecture of the current tax systems was put into place, it was not common for foreign source income to play anything but a marginal role. Foreign source incomes were seen as anomalies.

9. There is no example of a tax on capital income levied by a jurisdiction larger than a country. In fact, there is no example of any tax levied by a jurisdiction larger than the country, although the European Union has been receiving a share of the revenue from the value added taxes collected by the member countries.

The third essential element is the fairly wide dependence, despite various discrepancies, on the "global" approach to the taxation of both individuals and companies.[10] In both cases, it is assumed that the taxpayers put all their incomes, from whatever sources they originate, into one pot and report this total or "global" income to the tax authorities. The tax rates will then not discriminate among the components of that total, although they may differentiate among different income levels. This implies that *capital* income may be subjected to very high tax rates when a country imposes high, progressive rates on the global incomes of individuals and high rates on the income of enterprises. Finally, it is assumed that the tax authority will be able to verify independently the accuracy of the reported income.

Deep integration changes this picture. Even though taxation in a given territory remains the monopoly of the government that "controls" that territory, the tax authorities must deal with the growing importance of incomes earned in that territory by foreigners and with incomes earned abroad by its residents. This raises troublesome questions. For example, if taxation is, in fact, justified on the basis of benefit received by taxpayers living in the country, is it justified for a country to tax incomes earned in its own territory by foreigners? These individuals are likely to live abroad and will thus not benefit from the country's public expenditure (for schools, health, welfare programs, defense). However, if one assumes that government expenditure makes it possible or at least contributes to the earning of income,[11] then does it make sense for a given country to tax incomes earned abroad by its own citizens or companies? The point is that valid questions can be raised as to the justification, in principle, for treating all incomes equally regardless of their geographic origin.

More important, the globalization of income decreases the ability of the tax administration to verify the accuracy of the taxpayers' declarations. It is a safe assumption that tax administrations find it easier to control domestically generated incomes than foreign in-

10. By "global," I mean the total, comprehensive income of the taxpayers, be they individuals or enterprises. It does not necessarily relate to the geographic comprehensiveness of the income subject to taxation.

11. This is argued by several recent articles inspired by the "new growth theory." See the symposium "New Growth Theory" in *Journal of Economic Perspectives* 8 (Winter 1994), pp. 3–72. Of course, it is particular categories of public spending rather than the total that may contribute to growth.

comes. Differential economic opportunities across countries or regions and differentials in tax rates or in the efficiency of tax administrations will induce individuals and companies to invest and thus to earn incomes outside their territories. Assuming a continuation of recent trends, this phenomenon will intensify in future years, thus creating more and more frictions between an institutional-legal-administrative structure that remains tied to the principle of territoriality and economic activities that will lose more and more this national or territorial character. Except under implausible assumptions regarding the willingness and the ability of different tax administrations to exchange information, foreign income may at times become a synonym for evaded income.

Therefore, as the role of multinational corporations intensifies and the allocation of financial savings—managed by increasingly sophisticated, global money managers, relying on advanced technologies—becomes truly international, individual countries will be faced with two major problems: the increasing difficulty in verifying the incomes reported by their taxpayers,[12] and the increasing tax competition from other countries. Some countries may take advantage of the increasing globalization of the economy to attract foreign tax bases by decreasing their tax rates. Under these circumstances the key question is whether sovereign nations operating independently can continue to tax capital income in an integrated world economy.

The two problems mentioned previously may increase the bumpiness of the international playing field, thus inducing mobile capital to flow toward the low-tax jurisdictions. Or they may put pressure on countries to cooperate in exchanging information, in coordinating tax changes, or in harmonizing their capital tax systems. Over the long run, capital movements would tend to equalize the after-tax rates of return, implying, in the absence of similar effective tax rates, inefficiencies in the international allocation of resources and thus welfare losses for the world as a whole. This emigration of tax bases from high- to low-tax countries will reduce the tax revenue of some countries, reducing their ability to sustain their current expenditure levels, and it *may* increase the tax revenue of other countries. In the short run, the globalization of the financial market would make it easier for

---

12. Actually, part of the problem might be to discover the incomes *not* reported by the taxpayers.

the countries that experience revenue losses to finance fiscal imbalances because the same factors that reduce tax revenue will also raise the elasticity of the international supply of credit to any one country. Of course, financing of the deficit with resources borrowed from foreign creditors cannot be a long-run solution.

Before focusing specifically on capital taxation in an open and integrating world, it may be useful to relate the discussion of the previous pages to the lessons that could be drawn from the earlier discussion of the American federation. What factors have made it possible for American states to tax capital even though these states operate in a currency union with complete mobility of financial capital? Earlier, some of these were identified.

First, it was shown that the rates at which individual and corporate incomes are taxed are relatively low, and, more important, tax rate differentials, especially in an effective rather than a nominal sense, are small.[13] The taxes on capital incomes in the American states generate only a small fraction (about one-sixth) of the taxes on capital incomes imposed by countries. Second, it was shown that the tax bases on which the states' taxes are imposed are fairly similar across the states. Third, the similarity of the legal and accounting backgrounds for the states was noted. Fourth, attention was called to the complete and easy access to information on the part of the states' tax administration regarding the incomes earned by their taxpayers outside the states, that is, regarding the total incomes that taxpayers declare to the federal authorities.

Despite these facilitating factors, the states have not raised large amounts of revenue from capital taxation. They have also engaged in tax competition, which, by making the playing field uneven within the United States, has distorted the allocation of capital, has generated some inefficiency costs, and probably has reduced the level of revenue collected from these taxes. Finally, American states have relied on special systems for allocating the income of enterprises that operate in more than one state among the states.

---

13. It should be recalled that the combined revenue from the corporate income taxes of all state and local governments amounted to only 0.5 percent of personal income. The individual income taxes of states amounted to only 2.4 percent of personal incomes. Interestingly, taxes on capital incomes at the state and local level have been increasing rather than falling. They rose from 3.1 percent of total state and local taxes in 1962 to 6 percent in 1980. See Tax Foundation (1993, p. 189).

General Principles

There are two kinds of tax-induced distortions on which tax analysis has focused: distortions *within* countries and distortions *across* countries. The first is prominent when the playing field is not level within a country and the country has a closed economy. The second occurs when the playing field is not level across countries and the economies are being made progressively more open and international economic integration is occurring. Over the years, policymakers' and experts' concerns have been directed toward the first kind of distortion. In recent years, however, in part because of the role of multinational bodies (the European Community, the Organization for Economic Cooperation and Development [OECD], the International Monetary Fund, the United Nations [UN]) and because of the increasing attention paid by economists to these issues, there has been a growing realization that international distortions can be large and may require some policy response—either on the part of countries acting individually or acting in groups—to try to reduce them.[14] In the absence of such a response, the allocation of the world savings and capital might become progressively more inefficient, thus reducing world welfare.

If the playing field for investment were leveled, both within countries and across countries, and if there were no obstacles to the movement of capital so that it was free to flow everywhere, an efficient allocation of capital would result and a world rate of return to investment would come to be established. This rate of return would become the key reference point for all investments. Each investment in the whole world would be pushed to the point at which its rate of return would equate the world rate of return. As a consequence, both the gross-of-tax and the net-of-tax rates of return would be the same in all countries and in all sectors, and the difference between these two rates of return would reflect the average, effective tax rate on capital income.

However, as long as the rate at which capital income is taxed is not zero, the taxation of capital might encourage individuals to consume

---

14. For a useful discussion of general principles of international taxation, see Slemrod (1990b). For a first-rate and exhaustive treatment of the effect of taxation on multinationals, see Alworth (1988).

rather than to save. Thus intertemporal distortions would continue to exist even with this optimal allocation of capital. Conceivably this intertemporal distortion would depend on the level of the tax rate. The higher the tax rate, the lower the propensity to save. This implies that there are two fundamental aspects to the taxation of capital in an integrating economy: the extent to which the playing field is being leveled, and the tax rate at which the field is leveled. A less fundamental but still very important aspect is the extent to which the field that determines the rates at which personal savings are taxed is also being leveled.

In previous chapters, the tax implications of trade liberalization and of easier movements on the part of highly skilled or highly educated individuals were discussed. It was shown that the continuation of different tax regimes, in situations in which the countries' economies are becoming progressively more integrated, could generate large and probably growing misallocation of resources or revenue losses for some countries. A more level international playing field becomes more necessary the deeper the integration of countries' economies. The problems generated by uneven playing fields become particularly serious for capital taxation, be this the taxation of the capital incomes of individuals or the profits of enterprises. Because of the facility with which financial capital can now move internationally and because of the operations by multinational corporations in different countries, differential tax treatments of capital incomes across countries are likely to be exploited more quickly and more completely now than in the past and to induce potentially large capital movements.[15] These movements may have implications for the countries' tax revenue and may also generate welfare losses if *real* resources move just because of the tax rate differentials and not because of genuine differences in profitability.

Tax considerations are likely to influence the international allocation of saving and investment and the extent to which enterprises become integrated in an international context. Tax considerations may influence the distribution of branches or subsidiaries of multinational corporations. They may also influence the choice of the

15. As will be discussed subsequently, at least in some countries, these capital movements need not necessarily be accompanied by comparable movements of real resources. They may simply reflect accounting transfers in which profits are allocated to countries with low tax rates.

country where headquarters are established. These considerations may also influence the financing of investment—whether by equity or debt and domestic or foreign debt. In all these cases, the more deeply integrated the world economies become, the greater the distorting effect of nonharmonized taxation.

In recent years, in part as a result of empirical studies that have applied a methodology developed by Mervyn King and Don Fullerton to the measurement of effective tax rates on the income of enterprises, there has been a growing awareness that the size of these distortions may be large. (This methodology and some results obtained using it are discussed in the next chapter.) Although the replacement in many countries of cascading sales taxes with value added taxes and the fall in foreign trade taxes have reduced the tax distortions connected with the movement of goods, no comparable trend is visible on the capital side. However, the general fall in nominal marginal tax rates for both individuals and corporations and the fall in inflation rates in recent years have brought about some spontaneous reduction in tax rate differentials and, presumably, some reduction in the magnitude of tax-induced distortions. At the same time, however, both individuals and enterprises may have become more sensitive to the remaining tax differentials and more ready to exploit them.

Two general principles can guide the international taxation of capital incomes: the residence of taxpayer principle and the source of income principle.

As the name implies, the residence principle is based on the view that the country of residence of the person that receives the capital income (the investor) should determine the tax liability and collect the taxes. In other words, it is a principle ad personam that fits the tax liability to the person that receives the income. Thus if individuals reside in France, they owe to France the taxes on their total (world) capital income. Whether these incomes are generated domestically or in other countries is assumed to be irrelevant. By the same token, nonresidents are not liable to French taxes even when, in our example, they earn their income in France. This, for example, is the tax treatment of incomes earned in the United States and several other countries on bank accounts opened by "nonresident aliens."

For the taxation of the income of individuals, this principle, being ad personam, has the merit of making possible the imposition of

Residence of Taxpayer Principle

An individual resides in the United States but earns income from many sources:

United States	$ 50
France	20
Japan	15
Germany	15
Total world income	$100

The income taxed by the United States is $100. The $100 is subjected to the U.S. income tax. The individual will not pay any taxes to France, Japan, or Germany.

Source of Income Principle

An individual resides in the United States but earns income as above. Then each component of the total income is taxed separately by the country in which it is earned. Thus $50 is taxed by the United States, $20 by France, and $15 each by Japan and Germany.

It is obvious that the source principle is not consistent with global taxation but is more consistent with schedular taxation. In a global economy global taxation requires the application of the residence principle. This, however, is feasible only if the relevant information on foreign incomes can be obtained.

progressive and global personal income taxes whereby all the incomes of the residents of a given country, from whatever sources, are combined and subjected to the country's personal income tax. This principle can thus coexist with the use of global income taxation and with a progressive scale structure for that tax. It implicitly assumes that government expenditure, financed through taxation, benefits residents but does not contribute to raising the rate of return to capital invested domestically because nonresidents who have invested their capital in the country are exempt from the country's taxation.

The application of this principle by all countries would ensure what is called *capital export neutrality* because the allocation of investment among countries would not be influenced by the tax treatment of capital income in the countries that receive the investment and where the capital income connected with that investment would be generated. To the investors, the only relevant tax consideration would be the tax rates of the place in which they reside and not the tax rates in the countries where they invest their savings. If foreign investments generate higher rates of return than domestic investments, they will be chosen. However, as long as different countries tax the capital income of their residents differently, the residence principle would not provide a level field for the treatment of saving. Thus if all countries followed the resident principle but used different tax rates, capital export neutrality but not capital import neutrality would be ensured.

The source principle requires that capital income be taxed by the country where that income is generated and not by the country where the funds for the invested capital originated. Thus the source principle ignores whether the receiver of the income is a resident. To some extent, the source principle cuts the link between the income produced and the person receiving it. It is thus consistent with an approach to taxation that focuses on the object of the tax and depersonalizes the tax.

The source principle breaks the link between capital income tax and total personal income tax, especially when the taxpayer is a nonresident (and is thus more compatible with a schedular approach to income taxation). If the taxpayer resides in another country, and if the taxpayer's country of residence uses the residence principle, the possibility of double taxation is, of course, present. In these circumstances, the country of residence or the country of origin may choose to provide some tax relief to the taxpayer. In practice, this relief takes the form of a tax credit or a deduction of taxes paid abroad against the taxable income. A tax credit that rebates the tax paid dollar per dollar is, of course, more attractive to the investor than the deduction.

Tax treaties are aimed at alleviating this problem. There is now a dense network of tax treaties among countries. However, that network, even though it includes more than a thousand treaties, is far from complete because negotiating tax treaties is a lengthy process and because many countries have not seen the advantages to them of these agreements. The current treaty network is largely limited to industrial countries.

The universal application of the source principle would imply that the capital income of individuals living in a given country that was earned in different countries, and thus their investment, would be taxed differently depending on the tax systems of the countries in which they invested their money unless these countries harmonized their tax rates by, for example, agreeing on a common withholding tax rate. As a consequence, this principle would not provide a level playing field for international investment. Where investment would go would be influenced by the tax system of the host country. The lower the effective tax rate in a given country, the greater the inflow of investment. However, this principle would treat all foreign investors in a given country in the same way regardless of the tax rates in the countries in which these investors reside or in which the capital originated. By not interfering with the allocation of saving, the source principle would preserve capital import neutrality.

It has often been argued that the residence principle is preferable, on efficiency grounds, over the source principle. The reason is provided by Edward H. Gardner:

> From the standpoint of global welfare maximization, the choice between the two criteria depends on the degree of intertemporal substitution in consumption and of international substitutability of investment. With relatively low intertemporal substitution in consumption (that is, low interest elasticity of saving) and relatively high international capital substitution (that is, high elasticity of investment with respect to differences in after-tax rates of return), violations of capital-import neutrality should be less costly than a violation of capital-export neutrality.[16]

The residence principle may also be considered preferable on equity grounds because it is consistent with the application of a global and progressive income tax on all the incomes of individuals. In other words, it leaves a greater freedom of action to governments as to the

16. Gardner (1992, pp. 53–54). This argument is based on purely empirical (and possibly debatable) conclusions. As discussed earlier, the evidence in support of the conclusion that taxation plays a major role in inducing the movement of *equity* capital, which is the relevant one in Gardner's argument, is not overwhelming. Also, at least some economists would argue that the interest elasticity of saving may not be low.

use of the income tax for redistributional purposes. Because of its presumed superiority on both allocative and equity grounds, many experts have considered this principle to be a better guide to policy than the source principle.

Tax Havens, Tax Treaties, and Exchange of Information

Despite the support that it has received from tax experts and political and international institutions, the residence principle is not without shortcomings. These make it a less useful guide to policy than would appear on first consideration. Some of these short-comings are inherent to the principle itself, others to the way it interacts with established policies. It is somewhat ironic that the very developments that should make this principle more useful, that is, the process of world economic integration, are the same ones that set in motion forces that, in practice, reduce its usefulness or applicability.

First, even when the residence principle is followed, the tax payments to the country of residence might not be made for a long or even indefinite period at least for some taxpayers (that is, subsidiaries of transnational companies). The reason is that residence countries often allow the foreign subsidiaries of their national companies to defer tax payments until they repatriate their profits. Thus a residence principle that allowed indefinite deferment of the repatriation of the profits of subsidiaries would de facto reduce to zero the tax rate on these profits. Of course, this is not a criticism of the principle itself but of its possible application.[17]

Second, in a world in which tax havens are becoming progressively more popular, they may provide a convenient "tax address," and thus a convenient tax residence, for taxpayers who wished to reduce their tax liabilities.[18] This possibility will be particularly attractive for indi-

17. However, as discussed subsequently, the profits of corporations are generally subject to source-based taxation.

18. See Slemrod (1990a). As Caroline Doggart (1993, p. 1) has put it, "The advent of 20th Century systems of communication [has created] a new generation of mobile tax avoiders. . . . It consists of individuals and companies that are prepared to move their operating bases from country to country in search of low tax and capital growth." On the relation between tax havens and tax evasion, see also Organization for Economic Cooperation and Development (1987).

vidual taxpayers from high-tax countries who would be subject to high marginal tax rates on reported incomes in their countries. Some of these individuals may actually change their place of residence through migration. It will be attractive to individuals who have accumulated liquid assets from tax evasion or from illegal and criminal activities (for example, drug traffic) and who can claim, for tax purposes, a residence in a tax haven country helped by banking secrecy laws and other provisions of those tax haven countries. However, it will be also attractive to establish legal headquarters for some enterprises and, especially, holding enterprises, mutual funds, and other such institutions that can attract financial assets from individuals in high-tax countries and can invest them wherever the returns are highest. The earnings are channeled to the tax havens where they are subject to zero or very low tax rates. If the residence principle is fully applied, these earnings might end up escaping taxation almost completely.

The possibility of establishing residence or, at least, a "tax address" in a tax haven country clearly reduces some of the advantages of the residence principle. Capital export neutrality would still be achieved, because capital would still be channeled, or better rechanneled, to the countries with the highest prospective returns. However, the principle would no longer score so high in terms of equity because it would not coexist with the use of the global income tax for individuals where the savings originated. The country where the taxpayer truly resides and where the financial capital originates would lose tax revenue. If the countries that lose tax revenue react to this loss by raising taxes that impose high welfare costs or by reducing highly productive public spending, some of the efficiency advantages of the residence principle will be lost. At the same time, the total taxes on the income of enterprises would be affected if the dividends paid to the investors from the tax haven countries are taxed at lower rates than those paid to the investors who reside in the countries where the companies operate and the incomes are earned.

To qualify as a tax haven, a country must have low or no taxes on foreign source capital income, have political stability, be easily accessible, have a free exchange market, have banking secrecy, and have developed a good treaty network with important countries so that the incomes channeled to the tax haven country are not excessively taxed at the source.

Most tax havens are very small countries, not suitable as industrial centers.[19] Therefore both individuals and, especially, holding companies, mutual funds, and other financial institutions use these tax havens to channel to them the incomes earned elsewhere.[20] These allow them to escape the high rates to which these incomes would have been subjected in the real residences of the recipient of these incomes.

These tax havens do not have a large enough economic base to generate through their own economic activities the incomes received by those who establish residence in them. Rather they are simply convenient instruments for reducing the tax burden of some individuals or companies. Thus they play a larger role in allocating the world's taxable income than in allocating investible real capital. For the most part, and in the absence of special considerations, real resources will still go to the investments and the countries where they would have gone if the tax havens had not existed.[21] Thus the world allocation of real capital may not be greatly changed. What changes is the world allocation of taxable income. The world allocation of real resources would be changed much more if the tax haven countries had large economic bases and thus engaged in directly productive economic activities. In this case, real resource flows would accompany the financial resource flows to these countries. However, given that many industrial countries withhold taxes on incomes paid abroad and given that the withheld taxes tend to be higher for incomes paid to countries that do not have tax treaties, to the extent that these tax haven countries have developed tax treaties with some countries but not with others, there will also be some influence on the actual allocation of real resources.

A very important point and one that is often misunderstood is that it is *not* the existence of the tax havens that tends to lower the world tax rate on capital income, but the tax treatment of incomes earned elsewhere and channeled to the tax havens. If source base taxation were widely used, tax havens would not have much of an effect on the tax rates unless the tax haven countries developed large production

19. A comprehensive list of these tax havens is provided by Doggart (1993).

20. It is well known that Liberia and Panama have been convenient addresses for shipping companies. These companies register their ships in those countries to reduce taxes but, more important, to relax the constraints of various regulations.

21. This does not imply that the resources are allocated optimally because the playing field for real investment may still be bumpy.

bases themselves. It is the combination of tax havens with the application of the residence principle to some incomes that has this depressing effect on the world rate of taxation on capital income. The economies of the tax havens are too small to have on their own more than a very marginal effect on the world rate of return to capital. If large amounts of real resources were channeled toward these areas and were directly invested in them, the rate of return to these investments would drop very fast and would thus quickly stop the capital flow. However, if the residence principle is followed, if large numbers of taxpayers of important financial establishments claim residence in the tax havens or manage to transfer funds to them, and if the tax administrations of the home countries are incapable of preventing their taxpayers from establishing tax addresses there, the effect on the tax rates on capital income could be significant and the revenue losses to the countries that provide the capital could be substantial.

Incidentally, in terms of loopholes available to international investors to avoid paying taxes in their own countries, the American tax treatment of the saving deposits opened in American banks by "nonresident aliens" must rate among the most important.[22] This application of the residence principle by the United States has proved very costly in terms of lost tax revenue to many Latin American countries. In the 1970s and early 1980s, tens of billions of flight capital left Latin America to be invested in these accounts in banks in New York, Miami, Washington, and some other places. Over the years, these deposits earned billions of dollars that were not taxed by the U.S. government, because the owners of these accounts were not U.S. residents and were not taxed by the governments of the countries where the owners of these accounts resided because their tax administrations did not have the information to tax them.[23] The possibility available to Latin Americans to deposit their savings in tax-free accounts in American banks has put downward pressures on the tax rates that Latin American governments can levy on the capital incomes that individuals earn in their countries.[24] This is thus a classic

22. This treatment is available in several other countries. For example, countries such as Belgium, Denmark, France, Germany, Ireland, the Netherlands, Sweden, the United Kingdom, and Spain also generally do not withhold any taxes on nonresident savings deposits.

23. For a discussion of this issue, see McLure (1988).

24. I have often been told by Latin American officials that they were "forced" to levy very low tax rates on the dividends and interest incomes of their citizens because the latter could earn tax-free interest incomes in the United States.

case of "tax degradation" caused by the tax externalities created by other countries.

This example leads to the third shortcoming of the residence principle. The residence principle is feasible and useful only as long as the tax administration of the country of residence of the investor has the capacity to acquire the information about the incomes that their residents receive from foreign sources. Obviously, the information provided by the taxpayers cannot be assumed to be trustworthy, and more important, the taxpayers may not provide any information at all. Therefore, the tax administration must have its own way of getting it. For this, it will often depend on the willingness and the ability of other tax administrations to supply this information.

Many questions arise in connection with the issue of exchange of information. This issue has acquired, and will continue to acquire, fundamental and growing importance in an integrating world. The application of the residence principle and the attempt to tax income on a global basis will continue to be possible only if there is full and efficient exchange of information between tax authorities. Unfortunately, as Alberto Giovannini has summarized the current situation, there has been a "remarkable absence of cooperation among tax authorities in industrialized countries, mirrored by strategic use of bank secrecy laws to attract foreign tax evaders."[25]

Before discussing the question of exchange of information between tax authorities of different countries, it may be worthwhile to make a brief digression on double-taxation treaties. Most of these treaties concern income taxes and aim at eliminating or at least at mitigating double taxation. A significant number of such treaties covers only exchange of taxpayer information agreements between countries (mostly industrial countries). In a world in which source-based and residence-based principles of taxation coexist, these treaties try to establish rules that clearly divide the taxing jurisdiction between two countries with respect to incomes earned in one country by the residents of the other country. All treaties contain provisions for mutual assistance in fighting tax avoidance and evasion.

Although several "model treaties" have been proposed by various groups, the two most influential model treaties, which have provided the blueprint for most treaty negotiations between countries, are the

25. Giovannini (1990, p. 16).

OECD model and the UN model. There are some important philosophical differences between these two model treaties that are of some relevance for our discussion. These differences call attention to one area where strong pressures have been building up as a consequence of large capital flows. These differences have a bearing on the relevance or desirability of the residence and the source principle.

Suppose that two countries, A and B, both wish to encourage the free flow of capital across frontiers to promote economic efficiency. Suppose also that capital flows in both directions so that in each of these two countries some incomes are earned by investors who reside in the other country. In this case, the tax treaty should aim at eliminating or reducing double taxation by allowing the foreign investors to receive income without paying taxes (or by paying very low taxes) to the source country: The assumption is that these incomes will be taxed in the country of residence and that the exchange of information agreed in the treaty will make it possible for the residence country's tax authorities to get the information to tax these incomes. This is essentially the spirit that drives the OECD "model treaty," a model that has been very influential with respect to the tax treaties signed by OECD countries. It is a spirit consistent with the residence principle and with the desire to achieve the economic efficiency that comes with capital export neutrality. Because investment flows are expected to move in both directions, a priori questions about the fair allocation of tax revenue do not arise.

Suppose now that capital flows only or mostly in one direction. For example, the residents of country A invest in country B but not vice versa. Now a consequence of the application of the OECD model treaty is that, although country B will have the benefit of receiving foreign investment, capital incomes will flow mostly in one direction (from B to A). If B does not tax these incomes (following the residence principle), most or all the tax revenue will go to A. If B is now replaced with a typical developing country and A with a typical industrial country, it is easy to understand the reason why developing countries have been far less willing than the industrial countries to follow the OECD tax treaty model. The UN model, however, attempts to take into account the special situation of developing countries, and thus it leaves to negotiations the question of the (withholding) tax rates to be applied to capital incomes paid out of the countries. In a way, the UN model can be assumed to question the validity of the residence principle when capital flows move mainly in one direction.[26]

Globalization and increasing capital flows are likely to exacerbate the imbalances in the stock of foreign capital that goes to countries. Some countries will be net exporters of capital; some will be net importers; others will both import and export capital. If past trends continue, developing countries will be large net importers of capital, and many, but not all, industrial countries will be net exporters; the United States has become a net importer. The countries that are large net importers of capital may welcome the employment benefits that accompany these capital inflows but may not like the tax consequences under current tax rules.[27] If the incomes paid to foreign investors become large, the implicit tax "losses" will also become large. This situation is likely to lead to greater questioning of the residence principle and to the questioning, on the part of developing and other capital-importing countries, of the principles that have guided the OECD model treaty.

Now the possibility that the residence principle might be made feasible with increasing exchange of information among tax authorities, as several tax experts have argued, is dealt with more directly.

Exchange of information among the authorities of different countries concerning incomes earned in one country and not reported or underreported to the country in which the tax evaders reside would have to play a fundamental role if the growing integration of the world economies proceeds at the recent pace. This integration is leading to an exponential growth in foreign-earned incomes and thus to growing possibilities for tax evasion. There is more and more a feeling among some experts that foreign income may become a synonym for evaded income.

Bilateral tax treaties often carry provisions that permit one party to request information from the other party on the incomes that particular residents in the country represented by the first party may have

26. This issue arises not just for taxes on dividends but also for taxes on interest payments. For the latter, the question is whether the imposition of withholding taxes is reflected in the rate of interest that creditors demand when they provide the loans. For an empirical analysis of this last question with reference to withholding taxes on public interest accruing to nonresidents in industrial countries, see Huizinga (1994).

27. Actually, the attitude vis-à-vis foreign investment has been somewhat schizophrenic. See Tanzi and Coelho (1993).

earned in the country represented by the other party. To be able to make the request, the first party must have information to lead it to suspect that particular individuals are engaging in tax evasion. In general, the requested information concerns the taxes covered by the treaty. This is the so-called narrow exchange of information clause. However, information may also be provided for limiting tax evasion and tax avoidance in relation to taxes not covered specifically by the treaty. This is referred to as the broad exchange of information clause.

Exchange of information between tax administrations has grown as a result of the increasing number of tax treaties, especially among industrial countries, that has accompanied the growing globalization of economic activities. As already mentioned, the network of tax treaties has become particularly dense, with more than a thousand treaties now in existence. At the same time, agreements broader than those associated with bilateral treaties have started developing. An early example of these broad agreements and one that has influenced other attempts was the Nordic Mutual Assistance Treaty among the countries of northern Europe. This treaty was signed in 1972 and was amended several times until it was replaced by the Multilateral Convention on Mutual Assistance on Tax Matters, which came into force in 1991. Another early example is the 1977 EC Directive dealing with direct taxation. A potentially much broader, in terms of country coverage, new instrument is the Multilateral Convention on Mutual Administrative Assistance in Tax Matters. This convention is intended eventually to cover all OECD countries. It will begin to operate when at least five countries sign it. As of early 1994, four countries, including the United States, had ratified it. This multilateral convention is not limited to income taxes but extends to consumption taxes, estate and gift taxes, and some other taxes. Mutual administrative assistance includes exchange of information; the simultaneous tax examinations by two countries of the accounts of potential taxpayers; and assistance in the recovery of tax claims.[28]

Recent advances in the use of computers have reduced but not eliminated some of the purely physical obstacles that make it very difficult to exchange information and to use it. For example, in earlier years the Nordic Mutual Assistance Treaty often resulted in the

28. See Organization for Economic Cooperation and Development (1994); Pita (1993).

exchange of so many pieces of paper that they would fill whole rooms and would baffle the officials of the tax administrations that received them on how to use this information or what to do with it. Computer technology has at least reduced storage problems and the cost of transferring information from one country to another. However, several major difficulties remain. Some of these are legal, some are technical, and some are political.

Legal Difficulties

In recent years, increasing emphasis has been placed on taxpayers' rights, which may impose legal limitations to the kind of information that the tax authorities of one country can provide or are willing to provide to those of other countries.[29] This aspect becomes particularly important when the information may include trade secrets that may benefit the competitors from the requesting country. Promises that the information will be kept confidential may not convince the tax authorities of the country that will provide it.

Second, the obligation on the part of one country to provide information to another country may be confined to the taxes covered by the tax treaty or by the convention whereas evasion may be related to other taxes not covered by the treaty.

Third, the exchange of information is restricted to persons who reside in the countries covered by the treaty. If the tax evaders can claim a tax address in third countries, say, in a tax haven country, then the requesting tax authority may not be able to get the information.

Fourth, in several cases the tax authorities of the country that has been requested to provide the information may themselves not have that information and may not be able, for legal or even purely administrative reasons, to obtain it. This will be the case, for example, when special legal or administrative guarantees have been made to taxpayers. In these circumstances, and especially when under normal circumstances the country's authorities would not have the information (because of its own laws and practices), the country has no obligation to supply the information and no possibility of doing it even if it were willing to do it. In general, a country is not required to supply more

29. See, for example, Organization for Economic Cooperation and Development (1990). Taxpayers may have the right to prevent, through litigation, a country from providing information to another country.

information than it normally acquires under its own normal practice. In the case in which two countries have widely different practices, say, one has banking secrecy and one does not, the net result is that the information exchanged will be minimal.[30]

Technical Difficulties

Many countries do not keep their records in a format that lends itself to the easy identification of particular information. For example, they may store tax returns in ways that preclude easy access. In general, given their own constraints, countries will try to cooperate in providing the requested information, although some give low priority to such requests because of the need to deal with their own domestic tax evasion problems. This situation implies that the requesting country will need to send specific requests, such as the identification of specific tax evaders, based on its awareness that tax evasion is taking place.[31] However, these requesting authorities are likely to be aware of only the most egregious cases of international tax evasion or tax avoidance. In a fast integrating world, where foreign incomes are growing at an exponential rate, this approach is not likely to lead very far.

The alternative approach, by which countries would automatically pass on to other countries a large amount of information on all the foreigners who receive incomes from the country is often not feasible, and in any case, it is not likely to be very useful because the information may involve very large numbers and may be provided in a format that does not lend itself to ready use, especially by officers from other countries. Furthermore, the quality of the data may not be reliable. Such information is likely to overload the system and to prove useless. It must be recalled that resource limitations reduce dramatically the number of domestic returns that a country is able to audit—in the United States to less than 1 percent. Furthermore, some countries, such as Italy, still do not have single taxpayer identification numbers for use by their customs, their tax administrations, and their social security administrations. In these cases, exchange of information is

30. The limitations imposed by bank secrecy laws may be ignored in cases of criminal activities.
31. In particular circumstances, some countries may automatically send information on particular items or may spontaneously pass on specific information.

limited even within the country. Some countries, such as Japan, do not use taxpayer identification numbers,[32] and many countries, including the United States, still report significant degrees of tax evasion. If tax evasion on the part of their own citizens in their domestic activities cannot be eliminated, it is unlikely that these countries can be very successful in eliminating it with respect to international incomes.

Another important technical difficulty worth mentioning is language differences. In a world with literally hundreds of languages, in some instances differences in languages are likely to create major practical obstacles in these exchanges. Just imagine the Japanese and American tax authorities exchanging large numbers of documents. The idea that thousands or even millions of documents can be translated to make them useful on the part of the requesting authorities is not realistic. Anyone who has prepared a tax return that has at least some minor complications should be aware of how difficult the transmittal and interpretation of this information are likely to be.[33]

Political Constraints

In a world that is increasingly competitive, many governments may not show overwhelming enthusiasm in exchanging information on taxation when this information may discourage foreigners from investing in their countries or when the information provided may reduce the competitiveness of their country's exporters, be these the country's citizens or nonresident foreigners.[34] The policies of some countries, and especially of those classified as tax havens, have been directed at attracting investors and capital from other countries. Under these circumstances, one should not expect whole-hearted cooperation from these countries. These countries are likely to see this as a zero-sum game in which the revenue gains to other countries may imply revenue or investment losses to them.

32. As Ishi (1989, p. 323) has put it, "Heated arguments have taken place for or against introducing the tax identification number."

33. It may be worthwhile to add that in many countries the individuals who negotiate the tax treaties are not those directly responsible for the administration of the taxes; thus they may not fully appreciate the importance of these technical difficulties.

34. Definitions of terms such as resident and nonresident and permanent and non-permanent establishments differ among countries.

The perhaps sad conclusion of this brief survey is that it seems naive to assume, as some authors have assumed, that enhanced exchange of information among countries fully independent in their tax affairs is the instrument that will allow countries to cope with the exponential growth of foreign source incomes that accompanies the increasingly deeper integration of the world's economies. This is the fundamental difference between the experience of the states in the United States federation and the independent countries. It is the main reason why that experience cannot be a guide to what will happen in the world.

General Conclusions

In this chapter, several important questions connected with the taxation of income in an integrating world have been addressed, especially the question of whether the residence principle, generally followed and with an increased effort at exchanging information among tax administrations, could be the guiding criterion that would promote an optimal allocation of capital in a world undergoing deep integration. On this question, a somewhat negative conclusion has been reached.

In any case, the residence principle is not followed in any consistent manner across countries. For some important incomes (for example, the income of enterprises), countries normally apply the source principle. For other incomes (interest, dividends), they are not consistent with their treatment and often apply withholding taxes on foreign payments. For corporate income, it would be very difficult to apply the residence principle without at the some time allocating all the profits of an enterprise to the ultimate shareholders who may live abroad and may not be known. In the next chapter, some of these practices are looked at more closely.

Chapter 7

Allocation of Real Capital

*I*N the discussion of general principles that could guide the taxation of capital income in a world undergoing a process of deep integration, it was concluded that the optimal allocation of world capital, in the absence of significant externalities, would require that the same *effective* tax rate applies everywhere so that both the domestic and the international playing field for investment become leveled at the same tax rate. This condition would guarantee that capital would flow freely toward the investment opportunities with the highest, genuine, before-tax rates of return, regardless of where these opportunities are located, and would thus maximize world welfare. Taxation would not be a factor in determining where capital is invested. A major survey by Professor Michael Devereux, done on behalf of the Ruding Committee, concluded that, at least for multinational corporations, "taxation does appear to have a significant impact on the location of real activities."[1] As long as the effective tax rate is the same across countries, the effect of taxation becomes irrelevant regardless of the level of the rate.

In an optimal world, the rate of return to real investment must be the same as the rate of return to financial investment and, therefore, to saving. Furthermore, despite the conflicting empirical evidence about the relation between the saving rate and the rate of return to saving, economists generally believe that a high tax rate on the return to saving may reduce the propensity to save. In other words, a high tax

1. Devereux (1992, p. 116). The reason is that the effective tax rates remain widely divergent across countries.

rate on the return to saving (and thus on capital incomes) may introduce intertemporal distortions. Therefore, the *level* of the tax rate at which real capital is effectively taxed is also of some interest. A high tax rate may discourage saving (although the evidence for this is far from overwhelming) and thus reduce the world's investment. But a low rate may reduce badly needed revenue for many countries, thus reducing essential public services, and may make the tax system much less equitable.

The playing fields for real investment remain widely uneven both within countries and across countries. Within countries, preferential treatments to some sectors (through tax incentives and other policies) imply that investments in those sectors may be carried out even when the net of tax effective rate of return is low or even negative. Across countries, differential tax rates, the existence of tax havens, and the difficulty that tax administrations have in getting information on foreign source incomes imply that tax factors are extremely important in directing investment flows. When domestic incentives meet capital flowing in from tax havens, extraordinary results can be experienced.[2]

Figure 7-1 provides a visual sketch of the capital flows in a world undergoing deep economic integration.

The figure is largely self-explanatory. Capital flows out of set 1, which represents capital-exporting countries (mostly industrial countries but also some developing countries or territories, such as Singapore, Hong Kong, and Taiwan). Capital flows to developing countries (set 2), capital-importing industrial countries (set 3) and tax haven countries (set 4). To the tax haven countries it flows as financial capital. From the tax haven countries, capital is re-channeled, mostly to industrial countries. Capital income flows back to the capital-exporting countries and to the tax haven countries. Capital income may not flow back from tax haven countries to capital-exporting countries except in a clandestine and thus tax-avoiding way. The bumpiness of the effective tax rates on real investment income and the effective tax rates (adjusted for differential compliance rates) on the portfolio incomes determine the way in which saving and capital are allocated.

2. With practical examples, Valenduc (1994, p. 25) has shown that "when special tax regimes can be used and exempted profits can be repatriated with no or with a very low additional taxation to the parent company," sharply negative rates of returns before tax may still generate after-tax profits.

Figure 7-1. *Investment and Income Flows*

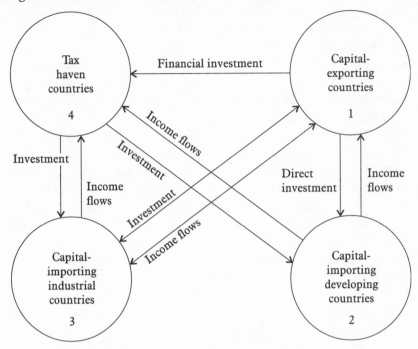

Some concrete cases in which differential tax rates have brought about major reallocations of capital follow. Some of these refer to personal income taxes and some to taxes on enterprises.

Personal Income Taxation: Housing

The rules on the deductibility of interest expenses by individuals are liberal in some countries, such as the United States, and restrictive in others, for example, Canada. A country that allows liberal deductions for nominal interest payments by individuals is likely to encourage them to spend beyond their current incomes, especially when the rate of inflation is significant and the tax rates are high.[3] This may, in turn, reduce the saving rate of the country and attract capital from

---

3. As I shall show in chapter 8, given some significant inflation and high marginal tax rates for individuals, the effective real cost of borrowing may easily become negative.

other countries. The rules that determine the treatment of interest expenses are at times complex. Furthermore, given the fungibility of money, individuals will be able to restructure their portfolios to borrow in connection with activities that allow for tax deductions while spending the borrowed funds for other purposes.[4] The Organization for Economic Cooperation and Development (OECD) has attempted to summarize these rules.

Table 7-1 provides a summary of the basic information for the year 1990. Some of the rules may have changed since that time. By and large, some countries provide very generous treatment of interest deductions whereas others provide much less generous treatment, and all countries do not distinguish nominal from real interest incomes and payments. Among the first group providing more generous treatment, one finds Denmark, Finland, Luxembourg, the Netherlands, Norway, Spain, Sweden, Switzerland, and the United States. As the table shows, these countries allow different deductions for loans on the principal residence and on the secondary residence, and for consumer loans. Recent legislation concerning interest payment deductibility and the fall in the rate of inflation and in the marginal tax rates have somewhat reduced the attractiveness of borrowing in the United States, but this country still remains among the most generous toward borrowers, mainly because of its generous treatment of mortgage payments.[5] Among the less generous group, one finds Australia, Belgium, Canada, France, Germany, Italy, Japan, and the United Kingdom. These countries either do not allow interest deductions for housing and consumer purchases or restrict them substantially. These distinctions will be used subsequently to separate the countries in table 7-1 into two groups.

The generous, or even overgenerous, treatment of nominal interest deductions, which sharply reduces, often to negative levels, the cost of borrowing, is likely to encourage consumption and discourage saving. In a world undergoing deep integration and in which financial capital can easily move across frontiers, that treatment is also likely to influence the international allocation of capital. Using the information

4. This has been clearly the case in the United States in connection with equity loans on housing.

5. For example, the combination of a nominal rate of interest on a mortgage of, say, 7 percent and an inflation rate of, say, 4 percent will reduce to a negative figure the real cost of borrowing for a home buyer who is taxed at the 1993 marginal tax rate and who lives in a state with personal income taxes. For further details on this, see chapter 8.

Table 7-1. *Deductibility of Interest Payments, 1990*

Country	Investment or business purposes[a]	Interest on loans for:		Consumer purchase[a]
		Home purchase or improvement		
		Principal residence[a]	Secondary residence[a]	
Australia	TA(B)	ND	ND	ND
Austria	TA(O)	TA(C)	ND	TA(C)
Belgium	TA	TA(O)	TA(O)	ND
Canada	TA	ND	ND	ND
Denmark	TA	TA	TA	TA
Finland	TA	TA(C)	TA	TA(C)
France	TA(B)	TC(C)	ND	ND
Germany	TA	ND	ND	ND
Greece	TA	TA	TA(C)	ND
Iceland	TA(B)	TC(C)	ND	ND
Ireland	TA(B)	TA(C)	ND	ND
Italy	ND	TA(C)	TA(C)	ND
Japan	TA	ND[b]	ND[b]	ND
Luxembourg	TA	TA(C)	TA(C)	TA
Netherlands	TA	TA	TA	TA
New Zealand	TA	ND	ND	ND
Norway	TA	TA	TA	TA
Portugal	TA	TA(C)	TA(C)	ND
Spain	TA	TA(C)	TA(C)	ND
Sweden	TA	TA	TA	TA
Switzerland	TA	TA	TA	TA
Turkey	TA(B)	ND	ND	ND
United Kingdom	TA(B)	TA(C)/TC(C)[c]	ND	ND
United States	TA(O)	TA(C)	TA(C)	ND

Source: Reproduced with permission from the publisher of Messere (1993, p. 274).

a. TA, tax allowance; TA(B), tax allowance deductible for interest on loans for business purposes only; TC, tax credit; ND, not deductible (or creditable); (C), subject to ceiling or maximum; (O), fully deductible but only against associated incomes.

b. In Japan there is a provision that allows a tax credit against income tax liability corresponding to 1 percent of outstanding loans related to home acquisition at the end of each year for a certain period.

c. There is no relief for home improvement loans taken out after April 5, 1988.

Table 7-2. *Net Household Savings as Percentage of Disposable Household Income: National Definitions*

Country	1985	1987	1989	1990	1991
Countries with most generous treatment of interest deductions					
Finland	3.9	1.8	−0.3	1.6	5.5
Netherlands	1.1	1.4	4.0	6.1	1.3
Norway	−2.7	−6.2	0.9	0.9	2.6
Spain	7.0	4.2	3.7	6.1	6.7
Sweden	2.3	−2.8	−4.9	−0.6	3.4
United States	6.6	4.5	4.1	4.3	4.9
Average[a]	3.0	0.5	1.3	3.1	4.1
Countries with least generous treatment of interest deductions					
Australia	7.7	5.3	7.5	8.8	7.4
Belgium	11.5	9.5	14.3	15.1	17.0
Canada	13.3	9.2	10.4	9.9	10.3
France	14.0	10.8	11.7	12.4	12.8
Germany	11.4	12.6	12.4	13.5	12.8
Italy	18.9	17.7	16.6	18.4	18.6
Japan	15.6	14.7	14.6	14.1	14.9
United Kingdom	10.6	6.8	6.6	8.3	9.2
Average[a]	12.9	10.8	11.8	12.6	12.9

Source: Organization for Economic Cooperation and Development (1993a, p. 146).
a. Unweighted.

available, a very simple test has been attempted to assess the possible effect on saving. The countries with more generous tax treatment of interest deductions and those with less generous tax treatment have been grouped separately.

Table 7-2 reports net household savings as a percentage of disposable household income for these two groups of countries. Admittedly, the grouping of countries reflects some personal judgment and might be challenged in particular cases. It follows the information provided in table 7-1 and it should largely capture the real situation. The expectation is that the countries that provide more generous tax treatment of interest expenses will have lower household saving rates than those that do not. The saving behavior of households in these two groups of countries is remarkably in line with the expectation. For the years indicated, there was a large difference in the average household savings rates of the two groups. If the difference in saving rates is attributable to the tax factor, given the deep integration of the world capital market and the facility with which capital moves, the conclusion must be that this feature of the tax system must be promoting major flows of capital across countries. These capital flows do not reflect real differentials in the productivity of investment but simply the influence of tax systems. They may thus be associated with large misallocation of resources on a world basis. At the margin, the last dollar invested in housing and in other expenditures is unlikely to have generated the same benefit across countries.

The size of the countries must play a role in determining the size of the misallocation of resources. If all the countries in the first group were small, the amount of world capital that they could absorb would be limited. However, the fact that the United States is among that group implies that the misallocation can be very large. This country can absorb a large amount of foreign capital, thus potentially driving up the world real rate of interest, before the lowering of the rate of return to investment in the privileged activity falls enough to stop the flow.

More speculatively, the low price of energy due to low excise taxes and the generous treatment of borrowing for housing in the United States may have created a combination that has been powerful in bringing about overinvestment in housing and in buildings in general. For sure, the average American consumes far more housing space than the average Japanese or European. Tax factors are likely to play some role in bringing about this result.

The differential treatment of interest deductions among countries has so far not been the subject of frictions. There has been no call for harmonizing or at least reducing the disparity in that treatment. It is to the credit of the OECD that it has paid attention to this issue by highlighting the divergence in the tax laws.

However, large capital movements, some possibly stimulated by these differences, have created some frictions among countries and some pressures, especially on those that were pursuing policies associated with fixed exchange rates. In a deeply integrating world the divergences in tax systems associated with the nonuniform treatment of interest deductions will sooner or later become an issue.

Taxation of Enterprises

The previous section focused on one important tax aspect—the deductibility of interest payments—that, in an integrating world, could bring about considerable misallocation of world capital and eventually frictions among countries. The issues in connection with that aspect were relatively simple. Unfortunately, this is not the case with the taxation of enterprises. Much of the real investment across countries is done by enterprises so that their role in allocating and in misallocating capital is large. For this reason, enterprise taxation has received much attention from lawyers, economists, and tax experts in general, as well as from governments and international organizations.[6] It is not possible to do justice to the complexity of this topic in the space available in this study. However, an attempt will be made to convey the essence of the difficulties and summarize the main issues.

Perhaps a good place to start is by going back to the example of the U.S. states. In that example, it was seen that corporations that operated in different states or in more than one state were exposed to the broadly similar set of accounting and legal rules that derived from the common historical origin. It was also seen that the tax rates applied by different states varied but not by a great amount, especially in an effective sense. Perhaps more important, the tax bases were fairly similar, having a common reference point, namely, the federal corporate income tax. Finally, there were no problems connected with different and changing exchange rates, with different inflation rates, and with limitations to the access to information. Yet the allocation of income across states for companies operating in more than one jurisdiction was a problem, and there was evidence of tax competition. The problem of allocating income among the different jurisdictions in which the enterprises operated was solved through formula apportionment.

For enterprises operating internationally, there are problems that do not exist in the purely American scene. First, because of the different historical and cultural backgrounds of the countries, accounting and legal rules tend to be very different; the tax systems

6. See, among others, Organization for Economic Cooperation and Development (1991b); Commission of the European Communities (1992); United Nations (1993, especially chapter 10); Hufbauer (1992); Siebert (1990); Jorgenson and Landau (1993); Kopits (1992).

differ with respect to rules concerning depreciation, evaluation of inventories, treatment of retained and distributed profits, and collection rules. This means that the definition of the tax base becomes very important and at times even more important than the level of the tax rate. Countries can compete through changes in the statutory rates or through changes in the elements that go into the determination of the taxable base such as depreciation allowances and methods of evaluating inputs used. Therefore, there may be large differences between effective and statutory tax rates. It is the effective rates that are important in the allocation of capital and that determine the extent to which the international playing field for investment is level.

When enterprises operate in several countries, and many now do, the tax complexities increase enormously.[7] These have to do largely with the need to allocate, for tax purposes, the income of the multinational enterprises among the states in which they operate. If the taxation of enterprises followed a residence principle, this allocation problem would not be necessary. In this case, the income would be attributed to the shareholders, in the case of full integration whereby all taxes are paid by the shareholders, or to the country where the headquarter of the company is maintained and where the company is registered.

However, countries are not willing to apply the residence principle to the income of enterprises. Rather, they think that they are entitled to a share of the profits of the enterprises that operate on their territory. Thus they apply the source principle. If they applied the residence principle to multinational enterprises, they would run the risk that the headquarters of the enterprises or the residences of their shareholders might be located in tax haven countries. To follow the source principle, when an enterprise operates in several countries, it is necessary to partition the total enterprise income among the countries in which the enterprise operates through its branches. This partition is difficult because different countries use different currencies, which may change during the year, and different accounting and tax rules. However, the allocation of income among different countries creates the possibility for the enterprises to use "creative accounting" to reduce their total tax payment. This, in turn, creates the need for tax administrations to watch carefully what enterprises do to prevent abuses. In this activity, the tax administrations badly need

7. For statistics, see United Nations (1993).

some of the information available to the tax administrations of the other countries in which the enterprises operate.

In their search for ways to minimize their total tax liability, the enterprises will take full advantage of legitimate possibilities that reduce the tax bases (such as tax incentives, inventory valuation techniques, or accelerated depreciation) and try to shift as much of the total profits as possible to countries that have low statutory tax rates, including, of course, tax havens. (They will also try to shift losses to the countries that have the highest tax rates.) In the process, the allocation of real investment may also be influenced by the tax rules that determine the tax base and, to some extent, by the statutory rates. However, the allocation of taxable income may be influenced mostly by the statutory rates: There is a great advantage to a company to show that a large share of its total income originated in a low statutory tax rate jurisdiction whereas the losses originated in the high-tax jurisdiction. In this whole process, tax incentives and tax havens will play a large role, especially for marginal investments. The combination of generous tax incentives combined with the possibility of attributing profits to a tax haven jurisdiction may make even projects with negative, before-tax rates of return profitable to the enterprise.[8]

The main techniques used by enterprises to shift profits to the low-tax countries are transfer prices; loans; the discretionary allocation of fixed costs, such as those for research, advertising, and general management, to particular countries; and royalty charges for the use of brand names and patents.

Available information shows that "a considerable proportion of cross-border trade of multinational enterprises (MNE) is within the same firm."[9] Some or much of this trade is in spare parts and other inputs of particular products that are not openly traded. For these items, it is difficult to determine what the market price (the arm's length price) would be. It is thus difficult for the government to establish the precise cost of these inputs. This gives the multinational enterprises the possibility of manipulating these prices to increase the costs and thus to reduce the profits in countries where the tax rates are high.[10]

8. See Valenduc (1994).

9. Dunning (1993, p. 386).

10. There is now an enormous literature on transfer pricing. See, for example, Plasschaert (1993); King (1994). For a good survey of the main issues, see Ikeda (1992).

Because intrafirm, but international, trade is growing very fast and much faster than even total international trade, the possibilities available to enterprises to manipulate transfer prices for tax advantages are increasing all the time. The tax authorities have thus been forced to intensify their surveillance of intercompany transfer pricing claims. At the same time, a growth industry of accountants, lawyers, and economists is assisting the multinationals in their discussion with the tax authorities. This is an area in which, regardless of what is done, difficulties are bound to grow with the growing role of multinationals and with the increasingly complex characteristics of the final products.[11] It should be understood that manipulation of transfer prices changes the location of taxable income and not the location of real investment.

The manipulation of transfer prices has become a major concern of international taxation. In 1992 the U.S. Treasury (Internal Revenue Service) presented a report in which it suggested that multinational enterprises operating in the United States were systematically understating their profits.[12] The state of California has been applying a special formula for the taxation of "profits" that it assumes originates in that state. This policy has been challenged by some European governments and by the Committee of Fiscal Affairs of the OECD. It has caused some friction, especially between the United States and European countries with major investments in the United States, such as the United Kingdom and the Netherlands. The issue was recently discussed by the U.S. Supreme Court, which decided that California has the legal right to tax foreign companies on a formula basis.

A multinational enterprise that wishes to reduce the share of its total taxable profits going to a particular country in which it operates can finance the capital investment of its branch in that country with loans rather than equity and in particular with loans from a low-taxation country, such as a tax haven. In this way, instead of receiving dividends, it will receive interest payments. The company that receives the loan will show lower profits because of the limited use of

11. The determination of the cost of inputs may be particularly difficult for complex, technologically advanced products. For example, a modern airplane has hundreds of thousands of different parts. Imagine the difficulties of assigning values to those parts when they are made in different countries and can be used only in that plane.

12. See Internal Revenue Service (1992).

equity capital and will thus pay little in taxes. Tax authorities have attempted to take measures aimed at reducing "thin capitalization."[13]

Through the allocation of fixed costs, such as research and development expenses, to certain branches or through high charges for the use of brand names and other patents, profits can also be shifted out of some jurisdictions into others, thus reducing the total tax liability of the multinational enterprises. "The opportunities for these types of tax arbitrage are likely to increase in the near future. The liberalization of capital movements raises the scope for avoiding taxes through purely financial transactions. At the same time, intracompany trade should grow. . . . Moreover, products for which transfer prices are especially difficult to determine [will] account for an expanding share of intracompany trade."[14]

The general feeling is that these maneuvers are reducing the tax liabilities of the multinationals and are thus reducing tax revenue from capital incomes for countries. This feeling has been particularly strong in the United States, where some statistics prepared by the Internal Revenue Service seem to back up this view.

Table 7-3 shows, for the 1981–90 period, taxable income as a percentage of total receipts and of total assets, respectively, for foreign-controlled and for U.S.-controlled companies operating within the United States. The data shown in this table indicate that foreign-controlled companies have consistently shown much lower taxable income than U.S.-controlled companies. This is true regardless of whether taxable income is related to total receipts or to total assets. Furthermore, the differences between the two groups of countries persist in time. It has been shown that these differences do not depend on the specific industry categories that attract foreign investors. Even when adjusted for industrial category, the differences between U.S. and foreign-controlled companies persist, pointing to the possibility that somehow, and possibly through the use of transfer prices, profits are being shifted out of the United States toward

13. Some manipulation is also associated with the interest rate charged for loans that are not made at arm's length. In January 1993, the Danish tax authorities fixed the annual rate for such loans, which can be reported to the tax authorities at the level of the discount rate of the Danish National Bank plus 4 percent. This was done to prevent the arbitrary shifting of taxable income out of Denmark through the exaggeration of interest rates. See Mikelsons (1993).

14. Tanzi and Bovenberg (1990, pp. 174–75).

Table 7-3. *United States: Taxable Income Reported by Foreign-Controlled and Other U.S. Domestic Companies, 1981–90*
Percent

| | Taxable income as a percentage of: | | | |
| | Total receipts | | Total assets | |
Year	FCC	OUSD	FCC	OUSD
1981	1.4	2.7	1.4	2.2
1982	0.4	1.6	0.3	1.3
1983	0.5	2.3	0.3	1.6
1984	1.0	2.7	0.8	1.9
1985	0.6	2.6	0.5	1.7
1986	−0.3	2.7	−0.2	1.7
1987	0.8	3.1	0.6	1.9
1988	1.4	3.7	0.9	2.2
1989	0.9	3.1	0.6	1.8
1990	0.2	4.0	0.1	2.1

Source: Internal Revenue Service (1992–93, 1993).

lower-tax countries or that foreign losses are being shifted to the United States.

The explanation that the profit differentials are due to income shifting has been challenged on four grounds: foreign companies have greater start-up costs; being newer, they have lower profits for earlier years in their activities; exchange rate fluctuations have at times depressed the earnings reported in the United States; and the share of taxable income in total assets is reduced because the book value of their capital assets is higher, compared to U.S. companies, because their capital has been installed more recently. Harry Grubert, Timothy Goodspeed, and Deborah Swenson have analyzed these issues and have concluded that they may explain about half the differences reported in table 7-3.[15] The other half may still be explained by transfer pricing and other similar tax avoidance factors.

Of course, income shifting aimed at reducing tax liability is not an activity in which only non-U.S. firms participate. U.S. companies that operate abroad may also be taking advantage of these possibilities. Two recent studies have provided some evidence on this issue. A

15. Grubert, Goodspeed, and Swenson (1993).

Table 7-4. *Revenue from Corporate Income Taxes in Industrial Countries*
Percent of GDP

Country	1970	1975	1980	1985	1990	1991
United States	3.7	3.1	3.0	2.0	2.2	2.2
Japan	5.2	4.3	5.5	5.8	6.8	6.2
Germany	1.9	1.6	2.1	2.3	1.8	1.7
France	2.2	1.9	2.1	2.0	2.3	2.0
Italy	1.7	1.7	2.4	3.2	3.9	3.8
United Kingdom	3.3	2.4	2.9	4.8	4.0	3.2
Canada	3.5	4.4	3.7	2.7	2.6	2.1
G-7[a]	3.1	2.8	3.1	3.3	3.4	3.0
EC[a]	2.3	2.3	2.5	3.1	3.1	3.0
OECD[a]	2.5	2.4	2.6	2.9	2.9	2.8

Source: Adapted from Organization for Economic Cooperation and Development (1993b, p. 80, table 12).

a. Unweighted average.

paper by Harry Grubert and John Mutti has shown that for U.S. companies operating abroad, the rates of return and the profit margins are higher in low-tax countries than in high-tax countries. This is what one would expect from income shifting.[16] David Harris and others have found that U.S. companies that had subsidiaries in low-tax countries showed lower overall U.S. tax ratios than U.S. companies with subsidiaries in high-tax countries.[17] These results are also consistent with income shifting.

The previous discussion about the effect of taxes on the allocation of real investment and of taxable income among different countries has emphasized the role of tax rates and tax bases in this process. As shall be seen, issues arise as to the differential rates; as to the different ways of defining tax bases, especially when countries provide tax incentives and special treatments to some forms of investment; and as to the ways in which individuals who own enterprises are taxed on the income they receive from them.

Table 7-4 provides some information concerning the tax revenue that countries derive from the taxation of corporations. These figures cover only corporate income taxes and thus do not reflect all the revenue that countries may derive from taxes, other than corporate

16. Grubert and Mutti (1991).
17. Harris and others (1993).

income taxes, connected with corporations. The table shows that, apart from the United States and Canada, which experienced falls in tax revenues (as percentages of the gross domestic product [GDP]) from these taxes, the other countries either maintained or even increased their shares from this tax over the twenty-one years covered by the table. The fall observed in 1991 is undoubtedly attributable to the steep recession.

Table 7-4 suggests that transfer pricing and other tax avoidance activities have, so far, not had a major effect on corporate tax revenue. The fall in tax revenue in the United States between 1980 and 1985 was the result of policies introduced by the Reagan administration in 1981. Other countries not shown in the table that experienced large increases were Luxembourg, Spain, and Turkey. Large decreases were experienced by Ireland and New Zealand.

The revenues from these taxes, expressed as shares of the GDP, vary by a large amount across countries. For example, in 1989 the ratio of the GDP varied from a high share of 7.5 percent in Japan and 8.4 in Luxembourg to a low share of 1.0 to 1.5 percent in Greece, Iceland, Ireland, and Portugal. In 1989, the last year before the recession started, the unweighted average for the G-7 countries was 3.7 percent of the GDP, reflecting a range from 7.5 percent for Japan to 2.1 percent for Germany. By contrast, the average for other groupings were 2.9 for total OECD, 2.6 for OECD Europe, and 3.0 for the European Community, all expressed as shares of the GDP.[18] Although the differences are not large, bigger economies tend to collect more taxes from this source than smaller economies, perhaps reflecting the difficulty that smaller countries encounter in taxing capital in an integrating world.

These figures refer to the taxation of "corporate" income. Thus they reflect influences such as the importance of the corporate sector in the economy; its profitability; debt-equity ratios; the efficiency of the tax administration; the effect of tax laws in the determination of the corporate tax bases, including forms of integration, if any; and the level of the tax rates. All of these factors vary considerably among countries. The last two are discussed here.

Table 7-5 provides relevant information on overall corporate tax rates and corporate tax revenue for selected countries. For most of

18. Organization for Economic Cooperation and Development (1993b, p. 80).

Table 7-5. *Corporate Tax Revenues and Corporate Tax Rates: Selected Countries and Years*

Percent

Country	Corporate tax revenue (% of GDP)			Corporate tax rate[a]		
	1980	*1985*	*1991*	*1980*	*1985*	*1991*
United States	3.0	2.0	2.2	49.2	49.5	38.3
Japan	5.5	5.8	6.2	52.0/42.0	55.4/45.4	50/47.3
Germany	2.1	2.3	1.7	61.7/44.3	61.7/44.3	57.5/45.6
France	2.1	2.0	2.0	50	50	34
Italy	2.4	3.2	3.8	36.3	47.8/36	47.8
United Kingdom	2.9	4.8	3.2	52	40	34
Canada[b]	3.7	2.7	2.1	42.4	51.6	50
Belgium	2.5	3.1	2.7	48	45	39
Netherlands	2.9	3.0	3.4	46	42	35
Spain	1.2	1.5	2.7	33	33	35.3

Source: Adapted from Organization for Economic Cooperation and Development (1993b, table 12) and from information in Commission of the European Communities (1992, p. 64).

a. These rates include the taxes imposed at local levels. Where two rates are given, the first reflects the tax rate on retentions, and the second reflects the tax rate on distributions.

b. For Canada, in 1991 the tax rate on the manufacturing industry was 35.7 percent.

these countries, there was a significant reduction in the statutory rates over the period shown by the table. The reduction in the rates was accompanied by a reduction in the dispersion in the rate levels even though significant differences remained at the end of the period between the lowest and the highest rates. These differences were high enough to play some role in the companies' decisions on where to invest and, perhaps as important, on where to show their taxable profits.[19] One significant aspect of table 7-5 is the lack of correlation between the level of the rates and the share of corporate income tax revenue in the GDP. For example, the United Kingdom with a rate of 34 percent, compared to a much higher rate for Germany, raises almost twice as much revenue as the latter. The comparison between the United States and Japan is also striking, even after taking into account Japan's higher rate.

Differences in the taxes on enterprises extend beyond the level of the statutory rates and include features such as the methods of

19. These differences were significantly larger than those prevailing among the states of the United States.

evaluating the cost of inventories; whether corporations pay property taxes, including net wealth taxes; the depreciation systems; the methods of payments and the length of the tax collection lags; the treatment of capital gains; the taxes on payrolls and the employers' contributions to social security systems; and the extent to which personal and corporate income taxes are integrated. These features tend to differ significantly across countries, some of them may influence the before-tax rate of return that investors require before carrying out investments. It is reasonable to assume that they also influence investment decisions. The extent of some of these differences is shown later in this chapter.

Of the other taxes collected from enterprises, other than those on corporate income, the most important are the employers' social security contributions and the payroll taxes paid by employers.[20] In several countries, these other taxes tend to be much larger in terms of revenue generation, than the taxes on corporate income. For the OECD area as a whole, they tend to generate about twice as much revenue as the latter. In particular countries, these taxes contribute several times as much revenue as the taxes on corporate income (table 7-6). With all its limitations (discussed below), table 7-6 cautions against overemphasizing the corporate income taxes. In fact, it shows that some countries that appear to be the most heavily burdened in terms of corporate income taxes, such as, for example, Japan, the United Kingdom, and Australia, are no longer in this category when all taxes collected from business activities are considered. However, some countries that appear to be lightly taxed under the corporate income tax—such as Sweden and France—appear to be much more heavily taxed when all business taxes are considered.

A major difficulty in assessing the importance of these other taxes in determining international capital flows is their incidence. One can object that table 7-6 links taxes that standard theory suggests fall on capital with taxes that standard theory suggests fall on labor. This table should therefore be taken as only suggestive. Consider the employers' share in social security contributions and the payroll taxes, for example. If the incidence of these taxes is on labor as tax experts

---

20. Because of the unanimous view that value-added taxes fall on consumers, these taxes are excluded. The inclusion of payroll taxes and the employers' share of social security contributions is questionable and is discussed subsequently.

Table 7-6. *Taxes on Business Activities, 1989*
Percent of GDP

Country	Corporate income tax	Other tax[a]
Australia	3.8	1.7
Austria	1.5	9.7
Belgium	3.0	9.3
Canada	3.0	3.6
Denmark	2.1	1.7
Finland	1.6	3.0
France	2.4	14.6
Germany	2.1	7.5
Greece	1.5	4.9
Iceland	1.0	4.2
Ireland	1.3	3.8
Italy	3.8	9.2
Japan	7.5	4.5
Luxembourg	7.5	7.7
Netherlands	3.5	7.6
New Zealand	3.6	0.7
Norway	2.4	8.2
Portugal	1.4	5.6
Spain	3.0	9.2
Sweden	2.1	16.0
Switzerland	2.1	3.8
Turkey	2.4	2.6
United Kingdom	4.5	5.7
United States	2.6	6.5

Source: Organization for Economic Cooperation and Development (1991b, p. 84).

a. These taxes include social security contributions paid by employers, taxes on payroll paid by employers, taxes on property paid by other than households, taxes on corporate net wealth, and other business taxes.

have often argued, then they substitute for higher wages paid to workers so that the cost of labor to employers would not be affected. If this assumption is totally correct, these taxes should not be included in table 7-6. In this case, they would *not* influence the return to capital and thus capital movements or even the relative competitiveness of countries: They would neither influence capital flows nor trade flows.

This conclusion has been challenged by governments and, especially, by businessmen who have complained about the high costs that these taxes impose on them. In other words, the latter have assumed that at least part of the burden of these taxes falls on them. In particular cases, accepting this argument, governments have assumed their burden. The fact that high unemployment in Europe is now often attributed to these taxes is an indication of the belief that they may reduce the rate of return to capital by raising the cost of labor. This may happen if minimum wages are too high (as, for example, they are in France) or if wages are too rigid downward, perhaps because of strong union power. The extent to which it happens is an open and difficult question. If these taxes fall at least in part on capital, the move toward a level field will need to take into account not just differences in the corporate income tax rates but also about differences in social security taxes and in some other taxes affecting enterprises. This is, however, a highly controversial question.

Another important point to recognize in connection with the taxation of corporate income is that the taxation of personal income is also relevant because corporations are owned by individuals and individuals pay some taxes related to corporate income, either through taxes on dividends received, through taxes on capital gains on the sale of their shares, or in other ways. If the individuals who own the corporations are totally rational and if the corporations are not managed by independent managers who ignore the welfare of the shareholders, it is the total combined taxes (both those collected from corporations and those collected from individuals on their incomes derived from the corporations) that should guide investment decisions.

In continental Europe, much more often than in the United States, enterprises tend to be run by the families that are the major shareholders. In the United States, professional managers often with limited controls on the part of the shareholders make the investment decisions. One could thus speculate that Europeans would tend to pay more attention to the total weight of enterprise taxation whereas Americans might focus more on the taxes that are directly imposed on the corporation. It is intriguing to connect this point with the fact that in the United States managers of corporations have shown little interest in the integration of corporate taxation with the taxation of dividends, whereas in Europe they have. The result has been a much greater integration in Europe of the taxes imposed at the corporate level with those imposed at the personal level, when dividends are paid out.[21]

The burden of the taxes on enterprises depends not just on the tax rates but also on the bases on which the rates are applied. In principle, these bases should be identical to the economic concept of income or profit and should thus be similarly defined across countries. In practice, the bases actually taxed differ widely from the theoretical bases and from country to country.

Factors that may bring about wide divergences between theoretical bases and bases actually taxed at the enterprise level are the relation between tax rules and financial accounting standards; the extent to which interest payments and other business expenses (including fringe benefits and salaries of executives) are allowed to be deducted; the treatment of trading losses; the treatment of depreciation costs; the valuation of stocks; the extent to which offsetting provisions for inflation are offered; and incentives that reduce the tax base rather than the tax rates.[22]

There is considerable variation across countries in the depreciation systems applied to machinery and buildings and in the methods of evaluation of stocks used in production. Substantial differences exist also in the granting of general investment reliefs. By and large, the G-7 countries do not grant these reliefs, but countries such as Austria, Belgium, Finland, Greece, the Netherlands, Sweden, and Spain do.[23]

Differences among countries in the taxation of enterprises can also be associated with other features. One is the collection lag, which, especially when the rate of inflation is significant, can provide advantages to companies that operate in countries where taxes are collected with long delays; for example, in the United Kingdom the collection lag is particularly long compared to that in the United States. Another is the tax treatment of capital gains at the company level, which can vary substantially, with some countries (Denmark, New Zealand) exempting capital gains, others (France, Ireland) taxing them at special rates, others (Australia, Ireland, Portugal, the United King-

21. For details see Messere (1993, pp. 342–63).

22. For a good discussion of these issues, see Messere (1993, pp. 332–38).

23. Detailed information on these issues is contained in Messere (1993); Organization for Economic Cooperation and Development (1991b); Commission of the European Communities (1992).

dom) providing an adjustment for inflation, and still others deferring the tax if the capital gain is reinvested (Austria, Germany, Ireland, Luxembourg, the Netherlands, Norway, Spain, the United Kingdom, and some others). Another difference is the extent to which countries attempt to reduce or eliminate the double taxation of dividends through the split-rate system, the partial dividend deduction system, the zero-rate system, or other ways of reducing the burden at the shareholder's level (partial imputation system, partial shareholder relief schemes, and the full imputation system).

In conclusion, in addition to the statutory tax rates, many other tax features, including the efficiency of the tax administration, can increase or decrease the attractiveness to foreign investment of a given country. The totality of these features determine the effective tax rates faced by investment in particular countries and determine to some extent the real investment decisions. Statutory tax rates are not the sole or even the most important tax influences on investment decisions. Differences in tax bases are equally important and so is the degree of enforcement.

Although statutory tax rates play an important role in tax arbitrage and in allocating profits among various branches of the same enterprise in different countries, it is the *effective* tax rates that have the greatest influence on where real investment goes. In other words, it is the effective tax rates that move real resources. These movements of real capital are likely to generate real welfare costs by inducing movement of resources toward countries with low effective rates even when these countries have lower before-tax rates of return to real investment, that is, even when these countries can use capital less efficiently than other countries. It is the before-tax rate of return that, in the absence of externalities, better measures the social return on capital.

Until now, the many ways in which the taxation of enterprises differs among countries have been discussed. All this information is interesting and useful, but it does not answer the question of whether, from a taxation point of view, country A is more attractive to invest into than country B. In other words, it does not answer the question of whether real capital investment will flow into country A or B for purely tax reasons. For doing this, a summary figure is needed, a kind of bottom line that weights into a single number all the effects coming from statutory rates, different incentives, different depreciation allowances, different systems of integration of corporate and personal taxes, and so forth. Only such a summary figure might tell whether the international investment field is leveled or not, and if not, by how much. However, one must be careful that the summary figure actually captures the features that are relevant to investors.

A summary figure that does *not* capture those features is the ratio of corporate taxes (or capital taxes) to the GDP. This is the information in tables 7-5 and 7-6. The problem with this figure is that it does not account for differences in the share of the corporate sector in the GDP or in the share of capital income in the GDP.

A better summary figure would be one that related capital taxes to before-tax capital income or corporate income tax to corporate income. This would provide an average effective tax rate. The ratio of capital taxes to capital income is difficult to calculate while the share of corporate income tax into corporate income ignores personal taxes on income derived from enterprises. Furthermore, these ratios reflect the average tax rates on total invested capital, whereas it is the taxes on the marginal investment that are relevant for capital movements.[24]

This leads to the cost of capital approach, especially as reflected in the methodology developed by Mervyn A. King and Donald Fullerton in 1984.[25] This methodology focuses on the concept of the *marginal* effective tax rate, which "facilitate[s] the representation of the economically relevant features of highly complex tax statutes in very succinct form. This has greatly enhanced the transparency of tax rules related to investment incentives." As Dale W. Jorgenson and Ralph Landau have put it, "A large part of the appeal of this approach is its ability to absorb an almost unlimited amount of descriptive detail on alternative tax policies."[26] In other words, this approach, in theory at least, provides the needed summary figure, or the bottom line, that would allow a comparison of complex tax systems and, as a consequence, would provide an answer to the question about the evenness of the international playing field.

The summary figures derived from the King and Fullerton methodology are shown either in the form of marginal effective tax rates or in the form of tax wedges. Tax wedges are defined as the differences between the cost of capital to the enterprise and the market rate of return on financial assets. More precisely, as Jorgenson puts it, "A tax

24. For an attempt to calculate these effective average tax rates on income derived from capital for the G-7 countries, see Mendoza, Razin, and Tesar (1993).

25. King and Fullerton (1984).

26. Jorgenson (1993, pp. 4, xvii).

wedge [is] the difference between the remuneration of capital before taxes . . . and the compensation, after taxes, available to holders of financial claims on the firm."[27] The cost of capital corresponds to the marginal rate of return that the enterprise must earn (before taxes) to be able to pay the market rate of return to a portfolio investor often assumed to be an institutional investor with a nonresident status.

If p is the before-tax rate of return and s is the after-tax rate of return that investors can get on financial assets, the tax wedge, W, is $W = p - s$.

The marginal effective tax rate, t, then can be expressed as the ratio of the tax wedge to the before-tax rate of return (the cost of capital), p.[28] Thus $t = W/p = (p - s)/p$.

To make these calculations, a lot of information is necessary about statutory tax rates and about the way in which the law defines tax income at both corporate and personal levels.

Since the time when King and Fullerton, building on earlier work by Harberger on the effective tax rate and by Jorgenson on the user cost of capital, developed this methodology, it has been applied several times to international taxation.[29] In the past three to four years, the International Monetary Fund, the European Economic Community, the OECD, and independent authors have attempted to measure, through the use of this methodology, the extent to which the playing field is leveled internationally.

Table 7-7 has been adapted from the recent book edited by Jorgenson and Landau. It combines the empirical results obtained by various authors on the nine countries shown in the table. All these studies followed the King and Fullerton methodology and even used Mervyn King's computer program. The table shows corporate tax rates, personal tax rates on corporate source income, and the combined corporate source income tax rates for the years 1980, 1985, and 1990. The results are shown as marginal effective tax rates rather than as tax wedges. The reader should compare table 7-7 with table 7-5 to appreciate the extent to which statutory corporate tax rates (as shown in table 7-5) can be misleading in assessing whether the international

27. Jorgenson (1993, p. 6).
28. For a good discussion of these concepts, see Commission of the European Communities (1992, especially pp. 67–92).
29. Harberger (1966); Jorgenson (1963); other authors, such as Alan Auerbach and Robert Hall, had also contributed to this literature. See Alworth (1988, chapter 6).

Table 7-7. *Corporate Sector: Overall Marginal Effective Tax Rates,*
1980, 1985, 1990
Percent

Country	Corporate tax rate			Personal tax rate on corporate source income			Combined corporate source income tax rate		
	1980	1985	1990	1980	1985	1990	1980	1985	1990
Australia	41.8	17.0	14.6	23.4	18.7	28.1	55.4	32.5	38.6
Canada	16.9	19.0	25.9	20.0	20.9	19.3	33.5	35.9	40.2
France	−28.8	−33.0	−33.4	74.1	75.2	65.4	66.6	67.0	53.8
Germany	15.2	9.9	4.6	32.9	31.5	28.6	43.1	38.3	31.9
Italy	−91.6	−95.4	−72.8	58.5	59.7	58.2	20.5	21.3	27.8
Japan	3.1	0.5	6.1	15.6	16.3	23.0	18.2	16.7	27.7
Sweden	−22.5	−5.0	1.0	37.9	37.0	27.8	23.9	33.9	28.5
United Kingdom	−31.4	21.4	28.0	30.7	17.2	13.8	8.9	34.9	37.9
United States	14.4	9.2	24.0	22.5	18.7	19.1	33.7	26.2	38.5

Source: Adapted from Jorgenson and Landau (1993, tables 1-1, 1-2, 1-3). For details the reader
must consult the basic publication.

playing field for investment is level. One important limitation of
table 7-7 is the assumption of a rate of inflation of 5 percent for all the
countries.

The first three columns in the table provide estimates of the
marginal effective corporate tax rates for nine countries and for three
years. The tax reforms over the period 1980–90 are reflected in the
changes in the reported rates. The table shows the enormous differences between, say, Italy, with sharply negative marginal effective
corporate tax rates, and Australia or Canada, with significantly positive rates. The negative rates are basically the result of investment
incentives included in the provisions for capital recovery.

The three columns at the center of table 7-7 show the marginal
effective personal tax rates on corporate source income. These rates
are all positive. Furthermore, some of the countries that favored
enterprises, as far as the taxes imposed at the enterprise level were
concerned, now sharply tax the individuals that receive corporate
source income. This is particularly evident in the case of France and
Italy, which impose very high taxes on individuals on their dividend
and interest income from corporations.

Concentrating on the last column of table 7-7, which combines the
marginal effective tax rates on corporations and individuals, it can be
seen that in 1990 the international investment field was far from even.

Table 7-8. Corporate Tax Wedges for Domestic Investment

Percent

Country	Average of each type of asset			Average of each type of finance			Overall average	Standard deviation
	Buildings	Machinery	Inventories	Retained earnings	New shares	Debt		
Belgium	0.4	-0.8	3.3	1.9	1.9	-2.2	0.4	2.5
Denmark	1.0	0.3	1.8	2.2	2.2	-1.8	0.8	2.0
Germany	0.1	0.2	1.9	3.8	-2.8	-3.6	0.6	3.8
Greece	0.0	-0.2	0.9	2.1	-2.3	-2.3	0.1	2.2
Spain	0.7	0.5	2.9	2.5	2.5	-1.5	1.1	2.1
France	0.4	-0.4	2.3	2.0	-1.5	-1.5	0.4	2.1
Ireland	-0.1	0.0	0.5	0.4	0.0	-0.4	0.1	0.5
Italy	1.7	0.5	1.3	3.8	-2.4	-2.4	1.0	3.1
Luxembourg	1.9	-0.1	3.4	2.8	2.8	-1.6	1.2	2.5
Netherlands	1.0	0.2	1.2	2.0	2.0	-1.8	0.7	1.8
Portugal	1.1	0.2	1.4	2.3	2.3	-2.1	0.7	2.2
United Kingdom	0.8	0.2	2.4	2.4	-0.3	-1.3	0.9	1.9
EC average	0.8	0.1	1.9	2.3	0.4	-1.9	0.7	2.2
Austria	0.4	-1.0	3.3	1.8	1.8	-2.4	0.3	2.7
Canada	1.4	0.3	2.6	2.7	0.5	-1.2	1.1	2.1
Japan	2.0	0.9	2.2	3.7	3.7	-2.6	1.5	3.1
Sweden	0.1	-0.5	1.3	1.4	-0.7	-1.9	0.0	1.7
Switzerland	0.7	0.1	1.0	1.5	1.5	-1.5	0.5	1.5
United States	1.6	0.2	1.4	2.4	2.4	-1.9	0.9	2.2

Source: Commission of the European Communities (1992, p. 81).

In France, the overall marginal effective tax rate on combined corporate source income was 53.8 percent compared to much lower rates (about 28 percent) for Italy, Japan, and Sweden. The rates were also relatively higher in Australia, Canada, the United Kingdom, the United States, and (to a lesser extent) Germany. According to these figures, the tax factor should push investment especially out of France and out of the other relatively high-tax countries. Table 7-7, however, also shows that the field for international investment has become much more even between 1980 and 1990 as far as the data reported in the table are concerned.

Table 7-8 presents an alternative and independently derived set of estimates, this time in terms of corporate tax wedges. It does so for three types of assets (buildings, machinery, and inventories), for three sources of finance (retained earnings, new shares, and debt), and for an overall average. Many industrial countries are covered by this table. The importance of distinguishing among assets is mainly due to their different depreciation treatments. The importance of distinguishing among sources of financing is due to the different tax treatments of, for example, debt and equity financing.

Table 7-8 addresses the following question: "Given a real interest rate of 5 percent in each country, what is the required pre-tax rate of return (the cost of capital) for different types of investment financed by different methods, and what is the difference between the pre- and post-tax rates of return (the tax wedge)?"[30] In a neutral tax regime, the required rate of return would be 5 percent, and thus the tax wedge would be zero. Table 7-8 shows that the tax wedges are not zero and are different among countries. The tax wedges for Japan, Luxembourg, Spain, and Canada are particularly somewhat higher than for the other countries. The tax wedges for retained earnings are much higher than those for debt, and the tax wedges for inventories are higher than for buildings. Clearly, the tax regimes are not neutral, so that distortions in the allocation of real resources are likely to occur.

The cost of capital approach was originally developed in connection with domestic investment decisions. It was extended by King and Fullerton to decisions involving different countries. This approach has been useful in driving home the point that the field faced by investors in a global market is far from level. It has also provided

---

30. Commission of the European Communities (1992, p. 72).

estimates of just how uneven the international investment field is and, indirectly, of how high the welfare costs associated with this unevenness in a world of capital mobility might be. Thus it has implicitly called attention to the need to level that field. In fact, the Ruding Committee used these estimates to make recommendations to the Economic Commission to bring some harmonization of corporate tax systems.

Before leaving this topic, it may be worthwhile to make a few remarks about some problems with this approach. First, for practical use, the approach needs to make several assumptions that inevitably influence the final quantitative results. These assumptions relate to the rate of inflation, to the real rate of interest, to who is the marginal shareholder of the corporation, to the way in which financial resources are assumed to be raised by the corporations, to the role of management as compared to the final shareholders, to the incidence of particular taxes, to what assets are bought by the marginal investment, and so on.

Second, given the complexities of the statutory tax systems, it is very difficult to take account of all the features that may have a bearing on the cost of capital. For example, an investment in Italy must pay attention to the regional location of the investment because of the tax incentives available in the south but not in the rest of the country.

Third, the results are calculated on the basis of the *statutory* tax system. Therefore, they simply assume away the problem of compliance. However, tax administrations are not equally vigilant or efficient across countries. Furthermore, as we discussed earlier, we know that the judicious use of transfer pricing, within-company loans, royalty charges, and other practices, can change the cost of capital, especially for marginal investments.

All these factors give the empirical results obtained from the use of King and Fullerton's approach a fragility that is worrisome. Different studies tend to report different results unless they are largely carried out by the same individuals.[31] Furthermore, the "summary figure" approach is useful in identifying the problem of the playing field that is not level, but it is not useful in pointing the way toward the reform

31. This is, in fact, the case in comparing the results shown in table 7-8 to those reported by the Organization for Economic Cooperation and Development (1991b, p. 100). Some of the same individuals were involved in both studies.

of the tax systems. Because the summary figure is the net result of many components of the statutory tax system, it does not provide guidance as to which of these components should be modified.

Still, the conclusion of these studies is important. When capital is free to move, the differences in tax wedges become much more important and potentially much more distorting than when capital is immobile, because in the former case the quantity of capital that can move is much larger. Therefore, the welfare costs associated with these differences can become much larger than in closed economies. This points to the need to try to eliminate or at least reduce these differences even if the tax wedges do not tell how to do it.

Within the European Community (European Union), there has been a lot of concern about the potential distortions identified above. Three basic objectives have guided the thinking of the Commission of the European Communities: to increase transparency and to reduce compliance costs across the European Union; to avoid tax competition that might result in sharp reductions in effective tax rates; and to minimize allocation distortions that arise from different effective tax rates.

In September 1990, the Committee of Independent Experts on Comparing Taxation (the Ruding Committee) was asked by the European Commission to consider the future of business taxation in the European Community. In March 1992, the Committee presented its recommendations. It advised against complete harmonization. But it recommended, inter alia, the establishment of a minimum tax of 30 percent on corporate incomes and the setting up of common rules for the computation of the tax base to avoid excessive tax competition and to increase transparency.

The reaction of the Economic and Financial Council and of the Commission to the Ruding Report was not exactly enthusiastic.[32] The commission stressed the importance of the subsidiarity principle and reacted negatively to the proposal to establish a minimum tax rate of 30 percent on corporate income. It stated that "the economic case [for this measure] seems to be less soundly based" and that "the 30 percent level proposed by the Ruding Committee would seem at first sight to be too high."

32. See Commission of the European Communities, "Commission Communication to the Council and to Parliament: Subsequent to the Conclusions of the Ruding Committee Indicating Guidelines on Company Taxation Linked to the Further Development of the Internal Market," Brussels, January 26, 1992.

Concluding Remarks

What conclusions can be drawn from the discussion of globalization and the allocation of international real investment? First, globalization makes investment more sensitive to differences in effective tax rates. Thus, capital tends to move faster, and in larger amounts, in response to these differences than was the case in the past with much closer economies. Second, *statutory* tax rates are not a good measure of the bumpiness of the international investment field. *Effective* tax rates are significantly influenced not only by statutory rates but also by rules that determine how the tax base is defined. Third, countries interested in attracting foreign real investment may be pushed toward providing tax incentives that reduce the tax base while maintaining the statutory rates. On the other hand, countries interested in attracting only foreign financial investment will tend to reduce their statutory tax rates. These latter countries are the ones normally considered tax havens. Fourth, differences in effective tax rates across countries reduce the efficiency with which international resources are allocated and thus reduce world welfare.

The empirical evidence available shows that, by and large, the international playing field for real investment is likely to have become less bumpy since 1980 because of the reduction in statutory tax rates, reduction in the rates of inflation, and reduction in tax incentives on the part of a few large countries such as the United Kingdom and the United States.

However, although the reduction in statutory tax rates has been fairly general, the broadening of the corporate tax base has been largely limited to a few, generally large, countries. Although no precise quantitative information is available, a widespread impression—especially on the part of experts and tax officials from smaller European countries—is that in several smaller countries a process of tax degradation, associated with a distortion of the tax bases and aimed at attracting real foreign capital, is taking place. For these officials tax competition is clearly a fact of life, one that in time will reduce tax revenue either through a further reduction of the statutory rates or, more likely, through the shrinking of the tax bases because of additional tax incentives.

This point takes us back to the key question of whether sovereign nations, operating independently, can tax capital income in an integrating world economy. The answer to this question is that they can, and will continue to be able to do so, but at a price. First, since the rest of the world does not tax real capital at zero rate but at some positive rate, a country, regardless of how small it is, will not need to reduce to zero its effective tax rate on income from real capital. Second, there are often location-specific reasons why companies prefer to invest in a given country rather than in other countries. Third, there will always be some domestic companies for which their country of residence is the preferred habitat, so that they will continue investing in that country even when, in principle, the tax rate in other countries may be lower. For all of these reasons the tax on the income of enterprises need not fall to zero. Of course, the price to be paid is that the degrees of freedom that policymakers once had in taxing capital income will be much reduced. Competition from other countries will push down the effective tax rate and reduce tax revenue. Competition will put in motion a trend that will over the long run reduce tax revenue from capital taxation unless some forms of tax harmonization prevent such a reduction.

There has been some discussion about the possibility that capital taxes could be harmonized so as to prevent this downward trend. These discussions have often focused on the statutory tax rates. The first problem with this approach is that it is politically very difficult to make countries agree on a given rate level. Conservative and liberal countries are unlikely to view the need for a given rate level in the same way. Second, there is no objectively determined rate level that can, in any sense, be considered optimal. In other words, there is no obvious reference point. In this area tax theory is not helpful: Whatever rate resulted from an agreement, it would be an arbitrary and politically determined rate. These two problems do not augur well for tax harmonization of statutory rates.

Although tax theory cannot settle the issue of the proper tax rate around which countries could reach an agreement, it can be very helpful in defining a proper tax base. It should be technically possible for a group of tax experts to define precisely the economic concept of corporate income. If an influential international organization or international commission promoted the concept of an optimal corporate income tax base, and certain powerful governments (say, the G-7) accepted such a concept, it might be possible at some stage to induce countries to reform their tax laws so that they all would tax the same base. In this way, tax competition carried through the erosion of the base would end. The proper definition of the tax base is a technical rather than a political issue, on which conservative and liberal governments may agree. Then competition would be carried out through the much more visible changes in the statutory rates. To achieve this result, it would be necessary to convince not only the top tax authorities in the countries in question but also the members of the parliaments that play a large role in determining tax policies. For this reason, one cannot be too optimistic about the prospects for such an outcome any time soon.

Appendix: Implications of the Marginal Effective Tax Rate Calculation

The marginal effective tax rate (METR) calculation summarizes a detailed analysis of the impact of taxes on the return from investment. The principle behind the formula is basic. Given a before-tax rate of return, an investment project generates a cash flow to which taxes apply, yielding an after-tax cash flow and an after-tax rate of return that summarizes the impact of taxes on the income generated by the investment. The METR is the difference between the before- and after-tax rates of return expressed as a percentage of the before-tax rate of return. In a similar manner, an after-tax rate of return could be specified and, based on the tax treatment of the project, a before-tax cash flow and rate of return calculated. The formula for the METR would be applied exactly as in the earlier case.

The treatment of depreciation, capital gains, debt, and other components of income in the tax system significantly affects the METR calculation. If deductible expenses equal real economic expenses, that is, if the tax base is equivalent to real economic income, the METR equals the statutory tax rate. In particular, tax deductions for depreciation of assets must equal real economic depreciation, and deductions for interest payments on debt must equal real interest costs. A difference between the METR and the statutory tax rate implies that the tax system fails to track real economic income accurately.

The METR can be calculated for different investment projects to illustrate how it can vary by type of asset, financing, and other factors. In this analysis, investment in each of three basic depreciable assets—

buildings, machinery and equipment, and vehicles—is examined. The investment projects were assumed to be in operation for ten years.[33] Replacement investment is undertaken each year at the rate of economic depreciation for each asset.[34] Such replacement investment holds the real value of each depreciable asset constant. At the end of the ten-year operating period, the assets are sold at a nominal value that equals their constant real value plus inflation. Sale of assets is included in the analysis to capture the effect of the tax treatment of capital gains. Inflation is taken to be 5 percent. The real before-tax rate of return is set at 15 percent. The rationale for this approach is that it reflects the calculation ex ante of the effect of taxes that an investor would make using a required before-tax rate of return. Three types of financing were examined: all equity, 50 percent debt, and 70 percent debt. The nominal interest for debt financing equals the real before-tax rate of return plus inflation.

The key features of the tax system used in this analysis include: corporate and personal statutory tax rates of 35 percent; personal taxation of dividends from capital investment; a straight-line depreciation schedule with annual rates of 5, 20, and 33⅓ percent for buildings, machinery and equipment, and vehicles, respectively; taxation of capital gains at the personal level as ordinary income with the base equal to sale price minus original cost; and deduction of nominal interest payments. This tax structure represents a stylized version of the tax systems in many countries, although it does not match precisely the system of any particular country.

METRs for the investment projects and tax structure heretofore described are presented in table 7-9. As this table illustrates, METRs vary considerably by type of asset and financing; they range above and below the statutory tax rate, as well as below zero.

The METR of 56.2 percent for all equity investment in buildings is substantially above the statutory rate of 35 percent, indicating that straight-line depreciation and the inclusion of nominal capital gains in the tax base overstate income from the investment relative to real

33. The calculation of METRs based on actual cash flows for individual investment projects can replicate the results of the King-Fullerton approach and is used here to illustrate variations in the METR by type of asset and financing that are obtained with the cash flow or King-Fullerton approach.

34. Economic depreciation rates were obtained from Hulten and Wykoff (1981). Specifically, these rates are 3.6 percent for buildings, 12.25 percent for machinery and equipment, and 30 percent for vehicles.

Table 7-9. *Marginal Effective Tax Rates for Investments in Buildings, Machinery and Equipment, and Vehicles*

Financing	Buildings	Machinery and equipment	Vehicles
All equity	56.2	39.5	30.3
50 percent debt	36.6	12.6	0.1
70 percent debt	23.3	−8.6	−22.9

Source: Author's calculations.

economic income. When this investment is 50 percent debt financed, the METR declines to 36.6 percent, close to the statutory rate. This decline follows from the effect of nominal interest deduction when interest payments overstate true interest cost in the presence of inflation. At 70 percent financing, the tax advantage of nominal interest deduction causes the METR to fall below the statutory rate.

For all equity-financed investment in machinery and equipment, the METR is 39.5 percent. The METR declines with debt financing and becomes negative at 70 percent debt, indicating that the nominal interest deduction produces negative taxable income that offsets positive taxable income elsewhere, thus resulting in subsidization of this investment through the tax system.

Straight-line depreciation for vehicles exceeds economic depreciation enough to reduce the METR below the statutory rate for all equity financing. The METR is essentially zero for 50 percent debt financing. At 70 percent debt financing, the project is substantially subsidized through the tax system.

Chapter 8

Allocation of
Financial Capital

THE previous chapter focused on the allocation of *real* capital in a world undergoing deep integration. This chapter deals with selected issues related to the flow of *financial* capital and the incomes that it generates.

Cross-border portfolio incomes may originate from deposits in banks made by nonresident depositors; from bonds (both public and private) held by nonresident bondholders; from dividends received from particular companies by shareholders residing in other countries; from dividends received by some companies from other companies; and so forth. Once again, this is a large and complex area, so only a few issues of particular relevance to this study are discussed.

The implication of the taxation of interest income in a world without frontiers for financial capital and with different tax rates is discussed, as well as some issues related to cross-border portfolio incomes in general.

Tax Treatment of Interest Income and Deductions

Four factors can distort the lending-borrowing decisions within a country and between countries: the rate of inflation, the level of the marginal statutory tax rate, the way interest incomes are taxed, and the tax treatment of interest expenses.

During the 1980s, the rate of inflation decreased in most industrial countries and is now generally low compared to the 1970s. Also, most industrial countries introduced reforms that reduced the level of

Table 8-1. *Inflation Rates and Top Marginal Tax Rates in*
Industrial Countries
Percent

	Inflation rate (consumer prices)		Top marginal tax rate[a]	
Country	1985	1990	1985	1990
Australia	6.7	7.3	60	48.3
Austria	3.2	3.3	62	50.0
Belgium	4.9	3.4	25	10.0
Canada	4.0	4.8	54	49.1
Denmark	4.7	2.6	73.2	57.8
France	5.8	3.4	26	18.1
Germany	2.2	2.7	54.5	53.0
Greece	19.3	20.4	0.0	25.0
Ireland	5.4	3.4	60	53.0
Italy	9.2	6.4	12.5	12.5
Japan	2.0	3.1	20	20.0
Luxembourg	4.1	3.7	57	51.25
Netherlands	2.2	2.5	72	60.0
Norway	5.7	4.1	40	40.5
Portugal	19.3	13.4	15	25.0
Spain	8.8	6.7	66	56.0
Sweden	7.4	10.5	50	30.0
Switzerland	3.4	5.4	45.8	43.8
United Kingdom	6.1	9.5	60	40.0
United States	3.6	5.4	54	36.0

Source: Inflation rates from International Monetary Fund (1992, p. 105); marginal tax rates from Organization for Economic Cooperation and Development (1991b, p. 78), and unpublished data from the Organization for Economic Cooperation and Development.

a. Refer to taxes on interest income for bank deposits. In some cases, these are "typical taxes" on interest income.

marginal statutory rates for personal and enterprise incomes.[1] However, both the rates of inflation and the tax rates remain high and different among countries. For 1985 and 1990, table 8-1 provides information on the inflation rates, as measured by changes in consumer prices, and on the marginal tax rates on interest incomes received by individuals.

For these years, the rate of inflation ranged from 2 percent in Denmark, Germany, Japan, and the Netherlands to about 20 percent

1. Reversing this trend, the United States has recently increased its marginal tax rate. It remains to be seen whether the influence that the United States had in the downward trend in rates will also be felt in this upward trend.

for Greece and Portugal, although for most countries the inflation rate was less than 10 percent. The marginal tax rates for interest incomes ranged up to more than 70 percent, although for most countries the rates were somewhat lower. These rates are applied to *nominal* (and not real) interest incomes, and nominal interest payments are deductible. This implies that inflation tends to subsidize borrowers and penalize lenders. A prevalent theory associated with the name of Irving Fisher and referred to as the Fisher effect suggests that, in general, the higher the expected inflation rate, the higher the nominal interest rate is likely to be. In fact Fisher theory assumes that the nominal interest rate rises pari passu with the rate of inflation. For this discussion, it is useful to assume that a Fisher relationship holds, so that the nominal interest rate is approximately equal to the real rate plus the expected rate of inflation. When the rate of inflation is high, the nominal interest rate in the Fisher relation tends to be significantly higher than the summation of the real rate and the rate of inflation. This qualification is ignored here.[2]

The *effective* marginal tax rates at which an individual's *real* interest income (that is, the interest rate net of inflation) is taxed when the marginal tax rates are levied on *nominal* rather than *real* interest income can be calculated. Assume that, in a world characterized by an essentially international capital market, an interest rate parity comes to be established whereby the world *real* interest rate is basically the same, apart from risk factors, in all countries and is largely determined by international factors. On the other hand, the domestic *nominal* interest rate is approximately equal to the world real rate, plus or minus the difference between the domestic rate of inflation and the world rate of inflation.[3] Then the international real rate can be used to solve the following equation:

$$ET = \frac{(R \times T)}{r} \times 100,$$

where R is the *nominal* interest rate within a country, which reflects, inter alia, the inflation rate of that country compared to the world rate; T is the statutory tax rate on the individual nominal interest

2. There is a large literature on this issue. A convenient reference is Tanzi (1984).
3. See Tanzi and Lutz (1993). The domestic nominal rate will also be influenced by the risk that the government will default on its debt. This default risk effect is ignored in this discussion.

Table 8-2. *Effective Real Marginal Tax Rates*
Percent

Inflation rate	Effective marginal tax rate[a]			
	0	20	40	60
0	0	20	40	60
1	0	25	50	75
2	0	30	60	90
3	0	35	70	105
4	0	40	80	120
5	0	45	90	135
6	0	50	100	150
7	0	55	110	165
8	0	60	120	180
9	0	65	130	195
10	0	70	140	210
15	0	95	190	285
20	0	120	240	360

Source: See text.
a. Figures assume that world real interest rate is 4 percent.

income; r is the world real rate of interest. ET is then the effective tax rate on real interest income.

Assuming inflation rates ranging from 0 to 20 percent, marginal tax rates ranging from 0 to 60 percent, and a world real interest rate of 4 percent, the *simulated* effective marginal tax rates shown in table 8-2 have been calculated. Ceteris paribus, the international financial market will tend to reallocate financial savings from the countries that find themselves in the southeast corner of table 8-2 (high inflation and high marginal tax rates) toward those in the northwest corner (low inflation, low tax rates). The table shows that the effective marginal tax rates on real interest incomes can easily exceed 100 percent. In this case the income tax becomes a capital tax. In countries where this happens, there will be little if any incentives for individuals who save to lend their financial savings within their own country. As a consequence, there will be a great incentive to invest in real assets or to take their savings out of the country, especially if they can be placed in one of those tax-free accounts for "nonresidents" that seem to be so widely available or in a tax haven country with bank secrecy laws. The incentive to invest in domestic financial assets will be much reduced.[4] Of course, individuals may still save and channel those savings toward real assets within their own countries if this can be done.

For the sake of completeness, it should perhaps be mentioned that there is a sizable theoretical literature that has argued that changes in actual or perceived tax rates on interest income from financial instruments, relative to tax rates on incomes from alternative assets, should affect the relationship between interest rates and real interest rates, given the level of expected inflation.[5]

The simple version of the Fisher relationship between the nominal rate of interest, R, and the expected rate of inflation, Π, is $R = r + \Pi$, where r is the real rate of interest. In the presence of taxes on nominal interest income, the theory states that the relationship should be modified to

$$R = r + \frac{\Pi}{1 - T},$$

where T is the tax rate on interest income. In this equation, the effect of Π on R is magnified by the existence of taxes: the higher T, the greater the magnification. Attempts at showing empirically the effects of taxes on nominal interest rates have generally not been completely successful, although some authors have claimed to have identified some tax effect.[6]

The tax treatment of interest expenses is also important in determining potential flows of savings across countries. Although the tax treatment of interest incomes affects the supply side of the market for funds, the tax treatment of interest expenses affects the demand side. When individuals (and enterprises) can deduct *nominal* interest expenses and the rate of inflation and the marginal tax rate are high, the

4. Unlike a closed economy, in which the main channel for savings may be real goods, a globalizing economy will offer a plethora of opportunities to escape the effective tax rates shown in table 8-2 through capital flight.

5. Three papers, written at about the same time, introduced this tax-adjusted version of the Fisher theory: Darby (1975); Feldstein (1976); Tanzi (1976).

6. See, among others, Tanzi (1980). The literature on this issue is both extensive and inconclusive. The theory itself has been qualified by pointing out that alternative investments (other than in interest-paying financial assets) may also be subject to taxes. Of course, if the international capital market is deeply integrated and if there are easy possibilities of investing abroad in de facto tax-free investments, this qualification becomes less significant.

Table 8-3. *Real Borrowing Rates*
Percent

Inflation rate	Marginal tax rate[a]			
	0	20	40	60
0	4.0	3.2	2.4	1.6
1	4.0	3.0	2.0	1.0
2	4.0	2.8	1.6	0.4
3	4.0	2.6	1.2	−0.2
4	4.0	2.4	0.8	−0.8
5	4.0	2.2	0.4	−1.4
6	4.0	2.0	0.0	−2.0
7	4.0	1.8	−0.4	−2.6
8	4.0	1.6	−0.8	−3.2
9	4.0	1.4	−1.2	−3.8
10	4.0	1.2	−1.6	−4.4
15	4.0	0.2	−3.6	−7.4
20	4.0	−0.8	−5.6	−10.4

Source: See text.
a. Figures assume that world real interest rate is 4 percent.

real cost of borrowing for individuals and enterprises can fall dramatically, even to negative levels.

Table 8-3 simulates some results, assuming once again a real world interest rate of 4 percent and the same range of inflation rates and marginal tax rates as in table 8-2. The real after-tax cost of borrowing, CB, for taxpayers who can deduct interest expenses from their taxable incomes at the top marginal tax rates is given by the formula $CB = R - \Pi - (R \times T)$, where R is the nominal interest rate, Π is the inflation rate, and T is the marginal tax rate. Table 8-3 shows that with a high marginal tax rate and high inflation rate, the real after-tax borrowing rate can easily become negative. In this case the income tax becomes a capital subsidy to the borrowers, as it was to many who bought houses in the United States in the 1970s. Under these circumstances, the demand for credit by individuals and enterprises within a country will rise, and especially within a deeply integrated international capital market, the country will, at least for a while, tend to spend more and to suck in financial capital from other countries. If the gross-of-tax real rate of return of the spending to which foreign capital is sucked in is lower than the gross-of-tax real rate of return on potential investments from which the savings are diverted, then there will be a misallocation of savings on a worldwide basis.[7]

The simulations in the tables show how important the rules are that determine the extent to which interest incomes are taxed and interest payments are deducted. If only *real* interest incomes were taxed and only *real* interest deductions were allowed, the world's allocation of financial saving would improve despite a continuing divergence of tax rates and inflation rates among countries.

The liberalization of capital flows, when combined with significant divergences in tax rates and inflation rates, creates large incentives for the movement of financial capital. These incentives are further magnified by the fact that the countries that receive the capital tend to rely on the residence principle (and thus they tend not to tax the interest income of nonresidents that this capital generates), whereas the countries from which the capital originates (because of administrative difficulties in identifying these incomes) are often unable to tax these incomes.

In 1989, the European Commission tabled a proposal for a common withholding tax on interest incomes among the countries of the European Community where this problem was seen as particularly acute. This proposal was strongly supported by France but was opposed by countries such as Luxembourg, the Netherlands, and the United Kingdom. As a consequence of this opposition, it was set aside. The alternative approach of routinely exchanging relevant information on interest incomes paid to nonresidents among the member countries of the Community was found to conflict with established banking and legal rules. So far, no common policy to deal with this problem has been developed by the Community (now Union). The existence of tax havens has complicated the issue because, even if the countries of the European Union would agree on some policy among themselves, the existence of tax havens and of countries outside the European Union that would not be party to the agreement would raise questions about the extent to which the agreed solution would solve the problem.

---

7. Of course, in time the country will run into balance of payments problems, which may lead to major devaluations. When this happens, those who have borrowed money abroad may find the cost of their borrowing (in domestic currency) considerably increased. However, those with high marginal tax rates and thus significant tax advantages may not be discouraged from borrowing by the possibility of devaluation.

There is no question that the situation described above has important allocative, redistributive, and revenue implications. Countries have been forced to introduce measures aimed at preventing large capital outflows, toward tax havens and toward lower-taxed countries, by lowering the effective tax rates on financial savings. This has been achieved in some countries by lowering withholding taxes (as in Belgium), in other countries by creating tax-exempt opportunities to their taxpayers (as in France and Belgium), or in some countries by relatively lax enforcement. It is obvious that these measures tend to reduce tax revenue and tend to affect the equity of the tax system by, de facto, replacing the concept of the global income tax by one that reflects a schedular approach to income taxation.

Taxes on Cross-Border Portfolio Incomes

Cross-border portfolio incomes originate from interest on deposits or bond holdings, from dividends paid by enterprises to nonresident taxpayers, and from other financial investments. In principle, the residence principle is supposed to guide the taxation of these incomes. The practice, however, is often not in line with that principle. For example, in many cases the countries in which the incomes originate (the source countries) choose to withhold some taxes on the payments made to nonresidents. In such cases, the tax authorities of the countries in which the investors reside may allow a credit for the tax withheld at the source, thus avoiding the double taxation for the particular income. However, this is not always the case. At times, the tax credit is provided for only part of the tax paid abroad, thus leading to heavier taxation of foreign source income as long as these incomes are fully reported. However, foreign investors may only pay the tax withheld at source when they do not report to their tax authorities the income received abroad and their authorities are not able to identify these incomes. In this case, foreign source incomes end up being more lightly taxed than incomes from domestic sources. In either case, the playing field for financial investment becomes uneven and the tax system becomes less equitable.

Examples of withholding at the source for incomes paid to nonresident investors by the countries belonging to the European Union are provided by table 8-4. That table shows that with few exceptions,

Table 8-4. *Taxes Withheld on Incomes Paid to Nonresidents, 1993*
Percent

Country	Banking accounts	Securities	Dividends
Belgium	0	10	15
Denmark	0	0	15
France	0	0	15
Germany	0	0	15
Greece	10	10	0
Ireland	0	0	0
Italy	10	10	15
Luxembourg	0	0	15
Netherlands	0	0	15
Portugal	15	15	15
Spain	0	0	15
United Kingdom	0	0	15

Source: Banca Commerciale Italiana (1993, p. 24).

Note: There are many exceptions to these general rates with respect to incomes paid to particular countries that may be subject to higher rates than those reported in the table. These exceptions are often linked to the absence of tax treaties.

countries generally exempt incomes earned by nonresident investors on banking deposits and on the holding of securities and bonds. Obviously, countries that receive these financial investments see benefits to them important enough to justify the application of the residence principle to these incomes. This, of course, gives a strong incentive to taxpayers to invest their financial savings abroad, especially if they can escape taxation in their country of residence.

However, most of the countries shown in table 8-4 withhold taxes at the rate of 15 percent on dividends paid to nonresidents. As was seen earlier, somehow countries are reluctant to apply the residence principle to incomes associated with the activities of enterprises, perhaps because there is a perception that the taxes on these incomes reflect some benefit connected with the activities and the spending of the governments where the enterprise is located. For all the incomes shown in table 8-4, tax treaties play an important role in the determination of the withholding rates (and to some extent on the willingness to exchange information) applied to incomes paid to nonresidents.

The treatment of these incomes by the authorities of the countries in which they originate also varies, whereby some countries subject them to global income taxes whereas others give them the particular treatment associated with schedular income taxes. Furthermore, for dividends the extent to which there is some degree of integration between the taxes levied at the enterprise level on the profits and those levied at the shareholder level on the dividends is also important for the determination of the tax burden on these incomes, the revenue received from the governments, and the extent to which the playing field is made level. Foreigners, of course, are unable to benefit from this integration. Available evidence indicates that the practices among countries vary widely. In general, there is far more advantage for a taxpayer to invest abroad in the form of financial investments than in the form of direct investments. Investment in shares generally benefits less than investments in interest-paying instruments,

The progressive removal of capital restrictions on the part of many countries is likely to make portfolio flows an increasingly important vehicle for tax evasion and tax avoidance. As technological innovation increases, the range of financial services that financial institutions are able to provide to foreign and domestic taxpayers will increase, making it more and more difficult for the tax authorities to control this process. Many of these financial institutions may operate from tax haven locations, making it even more difficult to control the incomes of those who use these institutions for their investments. Given existing tax rules, still largely based on the residence principle, it seems safe to predict that evasion will increase, and that exchange of information among tax authorities will not be able to do much to reduce this process. Smaller countries are, of course, more exposed to this process than larger ones. They can be major losers if they try to go against the trend or major gainers if they create conditions that make them attractive to foreign investors through manipulation of the tax system.

Over the long run there may be no alternative to the policy of imposing minimum withholding taxes on incomes paid abroad that are derived from financial investments. In this case the major issue will be the level of the rate at which the withholding tax will be imposed. This rate would have to be agreed upon internationally.

Chapter 9

Concluding Remarks

THE previous chapters have dealt with several tax issues that arise, or are likely to arise, in a world in which national borders no longer represent the sharp dividing line that once separated the economic activities of enterprises and individuals residing in different countries. Economic activities are now often international in scope, and goods, people, financial capital, real investment, technologies, know-how, and so forth cross national frontiers with a facility and a speed that would have been unthinkable a few decades ago. The best assumption that can be made at this time is that, barring a major catastrophe, this trend, which is largely driven by technological and policy developments, will continue in the future. By the time the next millennium comes, the activities of an overwhelming proportion of economic agents will have an important international component.

This internationalization of economic activities brings with it major implications for the countries' tax systems. The earlier chapters of this study have shown that various pressures have been developing among countries as a result of particular aspects of taxation. In particular, the degrees of freedom, in the choice of the preferred tax system and the desired tax rates, that a country once enjoyed have been reduced and will be reduced further in the future. This reduction is likely to be more important for small than for large countries, but it will affect all countries. In a world in which many economic activities are conducted on a worldwide scale, or at least on a scale that transcends national borders, these trends, if they continue to co-exist with differences among the tax systems of individual countries, will:

—Generate greater inefficiencies in the allocation of the world's capital because the allocation of capital will be significantly driven by tax considerations rather than by just rates of return before taxes and because the elasticity of the supply of capital for individual countries will be higher.

—Have implications for the effective progressivity of the tax systems if factors that are highly taxed in some countries, especially financial capital and highly skilled labor, can move to countries that impose lower taxes. Countries will pay a higher price than in the past if they impose effective marginal tax rates that are significantly higher than other countries. This is more likely to happen for factors residing in small countries than in large countries because the options available will be greater for the former.

—Affect the average tax level of some countries by forcing them to lower the tax rates for particular taxes unless they can increase taxes on inelastic bases; and more generally.

—Constrain the countries' policymakers in their choice of tax structures and tax levels.

Tax competition from other countries may force some countries into choosing tax structures (and, perhaps, tax levels) that their policymakers might consider less desirable than the ones they would have chosen if their economies had remained closed. In Europe, this effect has been given the not very complimentary name of tax (fiscal) degradation, although one should not infer from that name that the new systems are necessarily less efficient than the ones that would have been chosen in the absence of competition. Advocates of tax competition have argued that by forcing a reduction in marginal tax rates, competition will make the tax systems less distortionary and thus more efficient and will balance the policymakers' tendency to expand the size of the public sector and the level of tax rates beyond their economically justifiable limits. However, tax competition does not take place only through the lowering of the tax rates, even though this is the aspect of the issue that has attracted much attention in academic discussions. Tax competition may come mainly from changes or distortions in the tax bases that are less visible and more difficult to assess.

Tax competition will also provide incentives to some countries, and especially to some small countries, to become low-tax countries or even tax havens. If they can benefit by attracting large amounts of financial capital and by taxing it at low rates, they can increase their tax revenue without imposing higher burdens on their own citizens. Some countries may even attempt to attract consumers from other and especially neighboring countries by maintaining low excise taxes on particular products. This is another form of tax exporting.

A potentially disturbing feature of recent tax developments is the conflict that they are creating between traditional tax principles, which, as it will be recalled, were developed largely at a time when economies were relatively closed and thus economic activities were predominantly domestic, and the tax systems that will be feasible in a world in which economic activities become more and more international. Before discussing this aspect, it is worthwhile to mention that unlike other areas of economic activities, say, trade where the principle of free trade is widely if not universally accepted, the principles that have guided taxation have had far less support.

There was a time when most individuals earned income from only *one domestic* source and most enterprises operated within only one jurisdiction. As economies developed, an increasing number of individuals came to earn income from more than one source, although these were still largely domestic sources. The concept of "global" income tax was developed at this time and became a guiding principle for personal income taxation especially in Anglo-Saxon countries. The global income tax requires the aggregation into a total, or global, income of all the component income sources that an individual receives (wages, interest, dividends, profits, capital gains, gains from gambling, pensions). This total is then taxed with a rate structure that, in theory at least, makes no distinction among its components. Global income taxation thus requires that the tax authorities must have the capacity to verify whether the income declared by an individual, in countries where self-declaration is the norm, is effectively the total of all the components. In countries where there is no self-declaration on the part of the taxpayers, the tax authorities must themselves be able to aggregate the total income of the taxpayers. In part, as a consequence of the inability on the part of the tax authorities to perform this task, many countries, and not just developing countries, continue to use schedular systems in which each category of income is taxed separately, or at least they continue to have schedular features with respect to particular incomes (such as interest income or dividend income on wages, which are taxed with final withholding rates).

In recent years, the total or global income of an increasing number of individuals has been made up of not only various domestic sources but also of incomes derived from foreign sources. This raises the question of whether the tax administration of the country in which the taxpayer resides has the capacity and the means to verify the declaration of the taxpayers who have naturally a strong incentive not to report or to underreport especially the incomes earned abroad. The existence of tax havens with banking secrecy laws and an interest in attracting foreign capital on the part of many countries not technically classified as tax havens point to the possibility that many foreign incomes may end up escaping taxes in the country of residence of the recipients of the incomes. For example, much of the flight capital of the 1970s and early 1980s never paid income taxes to the countries in which its owners resided.

If the residence principle were strictly followed for all income and *if* information on taxpayers' incomes could be obtained by all tax authorities and exchanged efficiently and without restrictions, then global income taxation, with rates independently set by each country, would have a sure future. In this case, capital export neutrality would prevail because investors would be concerned only about the tax rates in the country in which they reside and, at most, they would engage in the drastic act of emigrating to lower-tax countries. However, this is not the case. The existence of tax haven countries that do not have an interest in sharing information with the countries from which they attract capital, and of banking secrecy laws in other countries, makes other countries unwilling to abide by this principle so that the latter impose taxes at source. Furthermore, the substantial legal, political, and technical limitations that exist on the exchange of information, even among non–tax haven countries, imply that it would be unrealistic to assume that the exchange of information can be the simple and only solution to the problems created by the developments described previously.

In recent years, there has been a growing intolerance on the part of some countries, and especially of the United States, toward tax evasion. Therefore, one can expect that political pressures will stimulate at least some countries to make greater efforts than in the past at limiting tax evasion by those who operate in their countries (both residents and nonresidents) and by their citizens when they operate outside their countries. They will urge or occasionally push other countries to cooperate in this effort. As with the fight against money laundering, the close cooperation by the G-7 countries and by other industrial countries can help promote this objective. In particular cases, some countries will expand their collaboration through the joint auditing of particular taxpayers. In some other cases, countries may even agree on the presence of foreign tax officials in their territory.

Still, all these actions, although worthwhile, are not likely to be very successful as long as there are sovereign countries or areas that benefit greatly from setting themselves up as low-tax jurisdictions at least for some forms of income. These countries will thus continue to attract (especially) financial capital that will be rechanneled to countries with large productive capacities and from which it can get a high rate of return. The income earned on these investments will then be channeled back to the tax haven countries. A tax address in one of these tax havens would thus allow some individuals to evade paying taxes in the countries in which they effectively reside. There is evidence of intensified competition among tax haven countries in providing tax advantages to those who invest in them. This competition may largely neutralize the effects of the intensified campaign against tax evasion.

It may be worthwhile to restate here a point made in an earlier chapter. The tax haven countries are often too small as real economies to significantly affect the world allocation of, and thus the return to, real investment. Often, they attract financial capital from some countries to invest it in other countries, or they provide a convenient address for receiving income earned from foreign sources. As long as the capital attracted by the tax havens and by the low-tax jurisdictions is not actually invested in them, the world allocation of real investments does not change and the world rate of return (before tax) to that capital does not fall. Of course, the allocation of taxable income does change so that some countries lose while others gain. However, the existence of tax havens tends to lower the world level of taxation. It is a different story when countries with large real economies lower their tax rates. In this case, the move of *financial* capital toward those countries is often followed by a move of *real resources,* thus leading to a potential misallocation of resources and a fall in the (before-tax) rate of return to capital if the additional investment in the low-tax country is strictly tax-induced.

No simple solution exists for this problem. However, if the attempts to reduce tax evasion through cooperative actions fails, it will progressively lead to a de facto second-best solution if countries abandon the concept of the global income tax and the residence principle and introduce schedular elements for at least some income (such as dividends and interests). These incomes would end up being taxed at source with final withholding flat rates, which would not discriminate between domestic and foreign taxpayers.

If this happens, the link between the taxpayers' global income and the tax that they pay would be broken. Some may see the breaking of this link as leading to a tax system that, in principle at least, would be less equitable or fair than the taxation of global income with progressive rates. However, in reality such a system would reduce the tax advantage enjoyed by those who channel their financial investments through low-tax or tax haven countries. In this case, the incomes paid to the tax haven countries would have taxes withheld on them, and the advantage of channeling investments through these countries would be reduced or even eliminated.

A shift from the residence to the source principle would, of course, have large allocative costs if the tax rates at which the taxes on incomes were withheld varied substantially from country to country. In this case, the international playing field could become quite bumpy, and capital export neutrality would be violated. If the taxes withheld at source became final taxes, then capital would tend to flow to the areas with the lowest tax rates, which might not necessarily have the highest before-tax rates of return. Some would argue that competition would tend to equalize the rates so that the efficiency costs associated with rate differences would be reduced or even eliminated. However, competition might tend to equalize the rates at too low a level, implying significant revenue losses for particular countries and the inability of these countries to sustain their level of public spending. Competition might also distort the tax bases, as explained in the previous chapter.

Economists have often argued that in a world with mobile capital, labor, particularly unskilled labor, will have to bear a greater tax burden because it is a less mobile factor of production than capital. Although the economics of this conclusion may be right, the politics of it is surely worrisome. It is difficult to conceive of a democratic society in which workers agree to be highly taxed while those who receive capital incomes are, even statutorily, taxed at low rates. The world just does not operate this way. In reality, the real incidence of the capital taxes might fall on labor if the statutory taxes on capital lead to the exodus of capital and thus to a fall in real wages. But this conclusion is not likely to impress politicians and to determine political decisions.

For enterprises, similar concerns arise. Many enterprises now operate on an international scale, with branches and subsidiaries in different countries. Some of these branches and subsidiaries may have been established keeping in mind the tax factors. Decisions by companies on where to locate and even on where to establish their headquarters or to raise their capital are now heavily influenced by tax factors and are likely to be even more influenced in the future.

For an enterprise with multinational activities, a big problem arises from the need to allocate its world, or global, income among the countries in which the enterprise operates. This problem has been increasing in importance, and given current and future likely developments, it is realistic to assume that its importance will continue to grow. This problem is particularly significant because, for enterprise income, countries have often relied on the source principle. The transfer prices used to do the allocation have often been challenged by the tax authorities of particular countries. And the concept of transfer prices to do the allocation has been challenged by various American states. Multinationals have been forced to hire an army of tax lawyers, accountants, and economists to defend the particular transfer prices they use. In some cases, advance pricing agreements have been negotiated to forestall future litigation. This has been the case between the United States and Australia with respect to Apple Computers.

The arm's length criterion for establishing acceptable transfer prices has often proved ambiguous or not very helpful. It may not be too far-fetched to predict that in a technologically evolving world, the allocation of income by the use of transfer prices may be subject to increasing challenges and may thus become progressively more controversial. Other allocation principles based on formulas may acquire more legitimacy than now. In the meantime, the conflict between the currently used principle of using transfer prices (based on arm's length) and the practical difficulty of determining objective transfer prices is likely to create the kind of frictions that came to a head in California and that led to the use of unitary taxation that is a formula-based allocation of profits. It should be recalled that the allocation of income of U.S. enterprises that operate in many states within the United States is done by formula and not by the use of transfer prices.

This discussion highlights the possibility that the world playing field may become less even and the need to promote more evenness. This, in turn, raises the issue of whether harmonization of rates might be brought about politically, either by agreement among the countries or by moral suasion on the part of some influential political institution.

Tax harmonization has proved very difficult for capital incomes even within the European Community. Various proposals for harmonizing the treatment of withholding taxes on saving, for example, have so far not been successful, but work is continuing within the Commission. For the Community, the lack of success so far has come despite the driving force provided by the work of the Commission.

For the world at large, there is so far no international institution that provides a kind of "surveillance" function over the developments in tax systems. There is thus no institution comparable to, say, the General Agreement on Tariffs and Trade or the new World Trade Organization for trade issues, or comparable to the International Monetary Fund for general macroeconomic issues, despite the fact that tax matters may become as important in relations among countries as trade matters. In fact, in some areas taxes may replace tariffs as instruments for manipulating trade for promoting the movements of factors of production.

For Organization for Economic Cooperation and Development (OECD) countries, the Committee for Fiscal Affairs provides a useful informative role, but that role falls short of what it needs to be on a worldwide scale (because only OECD countries are members) and on a political scale (because the role of the Committee is largely the diffusion of tax information and the discussion of technical issues). For European Union countries, the Commission provides more of the kind of political role that a world institution would need to play in taxation. There is no world institution with the responsibility to establish desirable rules for taxation and with enough clout to induce countries to follow those rules. Perhaps the time has come to establish one.

Comments

Joel Slemrod

> "Everything you know is wrong—and the things that you suspect aren't true, either."
>
> —Firesign Theater

Vito Tanzi's excellent book sounds the alarm that tax policymakers and tax experts must think globally. The combination of an increasingly seamless world economy and uncoordinated national tax policies raises important new questions regarding tax policy and, as the introductory quotation suggests, changes the answers to some old questions. The concluding chapter calls for a reexamination of traditional tax principles and for the creation of a world institution with the responsibility to establish and enforce desirable rules for taxation.

In the process of reaching these conclusions, this monograph accomplishes two impressive and important objectives. First, it collects an impressive amount of information documenting the fact that there are large differences across countries in their tax systems. These differences include the total amount of tax raised (as a fraction of the gross domestic product), which taxes are stressed and, for income taxes, not only the rate of tax levied but also how capital income is defined (depreciation schedules, inventory accounting rules, inflation

Joel Slemrod is professor of business economics and public policy, professor of economics, and director of the Office of Tax Policy Research at the University of Michigan, Ann Arbor.

adjustments), the extent to which the personal and corporate tax systems are integrated, the rules governing foreign-source income, and the deductibility of interest against nonbusiness income. Second, it thoughtfully considers the policy issues that are raised in a world of pervasive fiscal differences that is, at the same time, rapidly globalizing.

The pervasive tax differences have implications for the economic changes—including gains and losses—to be expected from globalization; also, globalization has implications for the likely future of tax policy. This two-way interaction raises the following three sets of questions:

—Are there large efficiency costs caused by international differences in tax systems? In part, such costs stem from the misallocation of real resources that follow tax incentives, which are similar to the costs caused by tariffs and other barriers to trade. There are also administrative and compliance costs, as national tax authorities try to defend their tax bases and individuals and multinational corporations try to minimize their tax liability.

—Does the uncoordinated political equilibrium produce a desirable outcome? Global economic integration places constraints on a country's tax policy by increasing the cost of certain policies such as taxing internationally mobile factors. What are the consequences of these constraints, both for national income and other objectives such as the redistributional potential of fiscal policy? Does the presence of fiscal externalities imply that national tax policies will be forced toward a "lowest common denominator," which may be appropriate given other countries' tax policies but which produces an inferior outcome from a global perspective?

—Is it desirable to have multilateral coordination or harmonization of tax systems? The answer to this question, of course, depends on the resolution of the first two sets of questions. If some degree of coordination is desirable, is it feasible?

Dr. Tanzi concludes this book with some very provocative answers to these questions. Along the way, he takes the reader through some fascinating terrain. He first looks at what lessons can be learned from investigating the federal tax system of "the free-trade area and the currency union that is the United States." Tanzi shows that there is significant variation across states in their tax systems; this variation is not as large as found across countries but, then again, U.S. states do not need to raise nearly as much revenue, relative to income, as do sovereign nations. Tanzi stresses their similarity rather than their differences, stating that the differentials in tax rates are not too high. This suggests to him that the states' policymakers have been concerned about the possibility that high tax rates may lead to tax exporting so that some competition-induced tax harmonization has taken place, leading to taxes that "do not get too much out of line" (p. 29).

Tanzi, though, rejects the application of this conclusion to the world, because of the special circumstances that describe the United States: totally free trade, no bank secrecy issue, a federal tax system that establishes a guideline for individual and corporate taxable income, and the absence of high multistage taxes such as value added tax (VAT). Just because uncoordinated state tax systems do not "get too much out of line" does not, he suggests, mean that there is not a significant problem globally. He does not, though, establish clearly at what point tax differences do get out of line or try to estimate exactly what the efficiency cost of the existing tax differentials is.

The chapter on indirect taxes, focusing on the VAT is of special interest to U.S. readers. The United States is virtually alone among industrialized countries in not having a VAT. Many academics and some influential politicians have supported the VAT as a replacement for some or all revenues raised by the personal and corporate income taxes. The politicians would be less enthusiastic if they read, and absorbed, the following sentences from page 47: "Because export prices do not reflect this tax, they are not distorted by attempts at manipulating trade. And because imports are taxed in the same way as domestically produced goods, they are not discriminated against." In contrast, many politicians are attracted to a VAT because they mistakenly believe it will provide exports with a competitive advantage. In fact, a VAT confers no more competitive advantage than would a retail sales tax (RST). Furthermore, a flat-rate VAT and a flat-rate RST are economically equivalent, putting aside administrative and compliance concerns and transition issues.

The problem is that, for tax policy matters, putting aside administrative and compliance concerns is usually ill-advised, and this caveat applies in spades when international tax matters are concerned. Most economists argue that, in a purely domestic context, administrative and compliance concerns favor the VAT over a RST, especially at a high rate of tax. In an international context, this choice is not so clear.

Until now, large differences in rates across countries for the multi-stage VAT were dealt with by having border frontiers. The European Union's desire to eliminate frontiers and failure to harmonize VAT rates has necessitated a complicated clearinghouse system to maintain the destination-base nature of the VAT.

Economic integration poses the most challenges for tax policy as it pertains to internationally mobile factors, usually taken to mean capital. In a nutshell, the problem is this: From any one country's standpoint, it is not appropriate to tax capital located within its borders (that is, on a source basis), because if capital is mobile, the tax will be passed on to the immobile factors (labor and land) as the capital flees, and the country suffers an avoidable excess burden due to the foregone capital. However, although it is not *desirable* to tax capital on a source basis, it is not administratively *feasible* to tax capital on a residence basis. It is simply more difficult to enforce a tax on one's residents' income, be they individuals or corporations, if that income is earned abroad.

The inadvisableness of taxing capital on a source basis, plus the difficulty of taxing capital on a residence basis, has led many observers, including Dr. Tanzi, to forecast the gradual deemphasis of capital taxation. Yet such a trend is difficult to observe in the data. Corporate tax revenues as a fraction of the gross national product have not fallen in the Organization for Economic Cooperation and Development countries, with the United States being an exception to this statement. Moreover, individual income taxes on capital have arguably risen in the United States during the past decade, so that a downward trend in the total tax burden on capital is not even clear in the United States.

Tanzi extends the mobile factor argument to the case of labor with exceptional talent, which, he argues, generates positive externalities. Citing recent work that speculates that the allocation of talent within a country has significant effects on the growth rate of the economy, he argues that a tax policy that causes these kinds of people to emigrate has a high social cost. Tanzi concludes that individual countries, especially small ones where the size of the market constrains the return to these individuals, should take pains to keep the top marginal tax rates on (labor) income from getting too high.

The effect of taxation on enterprises gets especially convoluted in a global economy. The variation in tax systems across jurisdictions can affect the location of real productive activity and, for a given pattern of real economic activity, where the profits of multinational enterprises are reported. most economic analysis considers these two dimensions separately, positing that real investment responds to the appropriate Hall-Jorgenson, King-Fullerton cost of capital, and that income shifting responds to cross-country differences in the statutory tax rate on corporate income. But these two dimensions of behavioral response are interrelated, because income shifting to low-tax jurisdictions is facilitated by having real operations located there. A correctly specified model would jointly determine real investment and income shifting, and the marginal effective tax rate on investment would be adjusted for how much income shifting is facilitated by that investment.

Scattered throughout this book are some provocative answers to the three sets of questions discussed above. For example, Tanzi says that it is unlikely that global income taxation can survive a process of deepening integration. The nomenclature is a bit ironic here. *Global* in tax parlance means comprehensive, including all sources of income without discrimination or preference. Tanzi believes that, in the face of globalization, a "global" income tax will be replaced by a schedular approach to income taxation, in which each source of income is taxed separately, enabling a country to impose lower taxes on more mobile factors. Until recently, a schedular tax system was judged to be the second-best choice of countries that lacked the administrative skill to enforce a global income tax. In the twenty-first century, a move from a global to schedular income tax would be an admission that the administrative superstructure does not exist in a global economy to enforce a global income tax.

Tanzi believes that there are large costs due to the current level of international differences in tax systems. He also believes that the pressure of globalization will pressure countries, ignoring fiscal externalities, to move toward flat-rate taxation of labor income and consumption, eschewing progressivity and thereby creating another dimension of cost as measured by social welfare. He believes that an international body to coordinate tax policy and enforcement, along the lines of the General Agreement on Tariffs and Trade, would be helpful to deal with both of these problems.

I am sympathetic with these views, although I believe that the process of moving toward the lowest common denominator fiscal system will be a very slow one and not an explicit one. In the current political climate, it is simply not feasible for most countries' governments to abandon explicitly the attempt to progressively tax all income, including capital income, and the labor income of the especially talented. The attempt to maintain the appearance of a progressive global income tax, although implicitly responding to the pressures of an integrating world, will in itself create inefficiencies and open up arbitrage opportunities to those willing to push the tax laws to their limits and make the true incidence of tax systems opaque.

Thus I suspect that tax structures will adapt slowly and in subtle ways to the pressures of an integrating world economy. For this reason, everything we know about taxation is not yet wrong but is a little bit more wrong every day.

References

Advisory Commission on Intergovernmental Relations. 1993a. *Significant Features of Fiscal Federalism, 1993.* Vol. 1. Washington.

————. 1993b. *Significant Features of Fiscal Federalism, 1993.* Vol.2. Washington.

Alworth, Julian S. 1988. *The Finance, Investment and Taxation Decisions of Multinationals.* Oxford: Basil Blackwell, Ltd.

Auerbach, Alan J. 1985. "The Theory of Excess Burden and Optimal Taxation." In *Handbook of Public Economics.* Vol. 1, edited by Alan J. Auerbach and Martin Feldstein, 61–127. New York: North Holland.

Banca Commerciale Italiana. 1993. *Tendenze Reali* 46 (July).

Bartik, Timothy J. 1989. "Small Business Start-Ups in the United States: Estimates of the Effects of Characteristics of States." *Southern Economic Journal* 55 (April): 1004–1018.

Baumol, William J. 1990. "Entrepreneurship: Productive, Unproductive, and Destructive." *Journal of Political Economy* 98 (October): 893–921.

Bewley, Truman F. 1981. "A Critique of Tiebout's Theory of Local Public Expenditure." *Econometrica* 49 (May): 713–40.

Bhagwati, Jagdish N., and John Douglas Wilson, eds. 1989. *Income Taxation and International Mobility.* MIT Press.

Bird, Richard M., and Charles E. McLure, Jr. 1989. "The Personal Income Tax in an Interdependent World." In *The Personal Income Tax: Phoenix from the Ashes?* edited by Sijbren Cnossen and Richard M. Bird, 235–63. New York: North Holland.

Bovenberg, Arij Lans. 1986. "Capital Income Taxation in Growing Open Economies." *Journal of Public Economics* 31 (December): 347–76.

Centre for Economic Policy Research. 1993. *Making Sense of Subsidiarity: How Much Centralization for Europe?* London.

Commission of the European Communities. 1992. *Report of the Committee of Independent Experts on Company Taxation.* Luxembourg.

Daly, Michael, and Joann Weiner. 1993. "Corporate Tax Harmonization and Competition in Federal Countries: Some Lessons for the European Community?" *National Tax Journal* 46 (December): 441–61.

Darby, Michael R. 1975. "The Financial and Tax Effects of Monetary Policy on Interest Rates." *Economic Inquiry* 13 (June): 266–74.

Devereux, Michael. 1992. "The Impact of Taxation on International Business: Evidence from the Ruding Committee Survey." *EC Tax Review* no. 2: 105–17.

Devereux, Michael, and Mark Pearson. 1989. "Corporate Tax Harmonization and Economic Efficiency." Report Series 35. London: Institute of Fiscal Studies (October).

Diamond, Peter A., and James A. Mirrlees. 1971. "Optimal Taxation and Public Production I: Production Efficiency." *American Economic Review* 61 (March): 8–27.

Doggart, Caroline. 1993. *Tax Havens and Their Uses, 1993.* London: The Economist Intelligence Unit.

Duncan, Harley T. 1988. "Interstate Cooperative Efforts to Enforce State Sales and Use Taxes." In *Proceedings of the Eighty-First Annual Conference on Taxation,* edited by Frederick D. Stocker, 93–98. Columbus, Ohio: National Tax Association—Tax Institute of America.

Dunning, John H. 1993. *Multinational Enterprises and the Global Economy.* Wokingham, Calif.: Addison-Wesley.

Feldstein, Martin. 1976. "Inflation, Income Taxes and the Rate of Interest: A Theoretical Analysis." *American Economic Review* 66 (December): 809–20.

Fisher, Ronald C. 1980. "Local Sales Taxes: Tax Rate Differentials, Sales Loss, and Revenue Estimation." *Public Finance Quarterly* 8 (April): 171–88.

FitzGerald, John D., and others. 1988. "An Analysis of Cross-Border Shopping." Paper 137. Dublin: The Economic and Social Research Institute.

Fox, William F. 1986. "Tax Structure and the Location of Economic Activity along State Borders." *National Tax Journal* 39 (December): 387–401.

Fox, William F., and Matthew N. Murray. 1990. "Local Public Policies and Interregional Business Development." *Southern Economic Journal* 57 (October): 413–27.

Frenkel, Jacob A., Assaf Razin, and Efraim Sadka. 1991. *International Taxation in an Integrated World.* MIT Press.

Galginaitis, Steven. 1992. "What Taxes Do States Impose on Business?" In *State Taxation of Business: Issues and Policy Options,* edited by Thomas F. Pogue, 3–16. Westport, Conn.: Praeger.

Gardner, Edward H. 1992. "Taxes on Capital Income: A Survey." In *Tax Harmonization in the European Community: Policy Issues and Analysis,* edited by George Kopits, 52–71. Occasional Paper 94. Washington: IMF (July).

Giovannini, Alberto. 1990. Reforming Capital Income Taxation in the Open Economy: Theoretical Issues." In *Reforming Capital Taxation,* edited by Horst Siebert, 3–18. Tübingen: J.C.B. Mohr.

Goode, Richard. 1976. *The Individual Income Tax,* revised ed. Brookings.

Gordon, Roger H. 1983. "An Optimal Taxation Approach to Fiscal Federalism." *Quarterly Journal of Economics* 98 (November): 567–86.

———. 1990. "Can Capital Income Taxes Survive in Open Economies?" Working Paper 3416. Cambridge, Mass.: National Bureau of Economic Research (August).

Grubert, Harry, Timothy Goodspeed, and Deborah Swenson. 1993. "Explaining the Low Taxable Income of Foreign-Controlled Companies in the United States." In *Studies in International Taxation,* edited by Alberto Giovannini, R. Glenn Hubbard, and Joel Slemrod, 237–75. University of Chicago Press.

Grubert, Harry, and John Mutti. 1991. "Taxes, Tariffs and Transfer Pricing in Multinational Corporate Decision Making." *Review of Economics and Statistics* 73 (May): 285–93.

Harberger, Arnold C. 1966. "Efficiency Effects of Taxes on Income from Capital." In *Effects of Corporation Income Tax*, edited by Marian Krzyaniak, 107–17. Wayne State University Press.

Harris, David, and others. 1993. "Income Shifting in U.S. Multinational Corporations." In *Studies in International Taxation*, edited by Alberto Giovannini, R. Glenn Hubbard, and Joel Slemrod, 277–307. University of Chicago Press.

Hines, James R., Jr. 1993. "Altered States: Taxes and the Location of Foreign Direct Investment in America." Working Paper 4397. Cambridge, Mass.: National Bureau of Economic Research (July).

Hinnekens, Luc. 1992. "Territoriality-Based Taxation in an Increasingly Common Market and Globalization Economy: Nightmare and Challenge of International Taxation in the New Age." *EC Tax Review* no. 3: 156–57.

Hufbauer, Gary Clyde, assisted by Joanna M. Van Rooij. 1992. *U.S. Taxation of International Income: Blueprint for Reform*. Washington: Institute for International Economics.

Hulten, Charles R., and Frank C. Wykoff. 1981. "The Measurement of Economic Depreciation." In *Depreciation, Inflation, and the Taxation of Income from Capital*, edited by Charles R. Hulten, 81–125. Washington: Urban Institute Press.

Huizinga, Harry. 1994. "Withholding Taxes and the Cost of Public Debt." IMF Working Paper 94/18. Washington: IMF (January).

Ikeda, Yuichi. 1992. "Treatment of Intercompany Transfer Pricing for Tax Purposes: A Survey of Legislative and Administrative Issues." Working Paper 92/77. Washington: IMF (September)

Internal Revenue Service. 1992. "Report on the Application and Administration of Section 482." Washington: U.S. Department of the Treasury (April).

———. 1992–93. *Statistics of Income Bulletin* 12 (Winter): 14.

———. 1993. *Statistics of Income Bulletin* 13 (Fall): 138.

International Energy Agency. 1993. *Energy Prices and Taxes, First Quarter 1993*. Paris: Organization for Economic Cooperation and Development.

International Monetary Fund. 1992. *International Financial Statistics, Yearbook 1992*. Washington.

———. 1993. *World Economic Outlook, October 1993*. Washington.

Ishi, Hiromitsu. 1989. *The Japanese Tax System*. Oxford: Clarendon Press.

Jorgenson, Dale W. 1963. "Capital Theory and Investment Behavior." *American Economic Review* 53 (May): 247–59.

———. 1993. "Introduction and Summary." In *Tax Reform and the Cost of Capital: An International Comparison*, edited by Dale W. Jorgenson and Ralph Landau, 1–56. Brookings.

Jorgenson, Dale W., and Ralph Landau, eds. 1993. *Tax Reform and the Cost of Capital: An International Comparison*. Brookings.

Kanbur, Ravi, and Michael Keen. 1993. "Jeux Sans Frontiéres: Tax Competition and Tax Coordination when Countries Differ in Size." *American Economic Review* 83 (September): 877–92.

Keen, Michael. 1993. "The Welfare Economics of Tax Coordination in the European Community: A Survey." *Fiscal Studies* 14 (2): 15–36.

Kieschnick, M. 1981. "Taxes and Growth: Business Incentives and Development." Washington: Council of State-Planning Agencies.

King, Elizabeth A. 1994. *Transfer Pricing and Valuation in Corporate Taxation: Federal Legislation vs. Administrative Practice.* Boston: Kluwer Academic Publishers.

King, Mervyn A., and Don Fullerton. 1984. *The Taxation of Income from Capital.* University of Chicago Press.

Kopits, George, ed. 1992. *Tax Harmonization in the European Community: Policy Issues and Analysis.* Occasional Paper 94. Washington: IMF (July).

KPMG Peat Marwick, Economic Policy Group. 1993. "Effects of Cross-Border Sales on Economic Activity and State Revenues: A Case Study of Tobacco Excise Taxes in Massachusetts, New York City, and Surrounding Areas." Background Paper 3. Washington: Tax Foundation (January).

Ledebur, L.C., and W.W. Hamilton. 1986. "Tax Concessions in State and Local Economic Development." Aslan Economic Development Series. McLean, Va.: Aslan Press.

Lipsey, Robert E., and Irving B. Kravis. 1987. "Is the U.S. a Spendthrift Nation?" Working Paper 2274. Washington: National Bureau of Economic Research (June).

McLure, Charles E., Jr. 1986a. *Economic Perspectives on State Taxation of Multijurisdictional Corporations.* Arlington, Va.: Tax Analysts.

―――. 1986b. "Tax Competition: Is What's Good for the Private Goose Also Good for the Public Gander?" *National Tax Journal* 39 (September): 341–48.

―――. 1988. "U.S. Tax Laws and Capital Flight from Latin America." Working Papers in Economics E-88-21. Palo Alto, Calif.: Hoover Institution and Stanford University (April).

Mendoza, Enrique G., Assaf Razin, and Linda L. Tesar. 1993. "An International Comparison of Tax Systems in Industrial Countries." In *Staff Studies for the World Economic Outlook,* 86–105. Washington: IMF (December).

Messere, K.C. 1993. *Tax Policy in OECD Countries: Choices and Conflicts.* Amsterdam: IBFD Publications.

Mikelsons, Robert. 1993. "Denmark: Interest on Non Arms'-Length Loans." *World Tax Report* 18 (March): 43.

Mikesell, John L. 1970. "Central Cities and Sales Tax Differentials: The Border City Problem." *National Tax Journal* 23 (June): 206–14.

Mintz, Jack M. 1992. "Is There a Future for Capital Income Taxation?" Working Paper 108. Paris: Organization for Economic Co-operation and Development.

Murphy, Kevin M., Andrei Shleifer, and Robert W. Vishny. 1991. "The Allocation of Talent: Implications for Growth." *Quarterly Journal of Economics* 106 (May): 503–30.

Musgrave, Richard A. 1959. *The Theory of Public Finance: A Study in Public Economy.* McGraw-Hill Book Company.

Organization for Economic Cooperation and Development (OECD). 1987. *International Tax Avoidance and Evasion: Four Related Studies.* Paris.

―――. 1990. *Taxpayers' Rights and Obligations: A Survey of the Legal Situation in OECD Countries.* Paris.

―――. 1991a. *Revenue Statistics of OECD Countries.* Paris.

————. 1991b. *Taxing Profits in a Global Economy: Domestic and International Issues.* Paris.

————. 1993a. *Economic Outlook* no. 54. Paris (December).

————. 1993b. *Revenue Statistics of OECD Member Countries, 1965–1992.* Paris.

————. 1993c. *The Tax/Benefit Position of Production Workers.* Paris.

————. 1994. *Tax Information Exchange between OECD Member Countries: A Survey of Current Practices.* Paris.

Papke, Leslie E. 1987. "Subnational Taxation and Capital Mobility: Estimates of Tax Price Elasticities." *National Tax Journal* 40 (June): 191–204.

————. 1991. "Interstate Business Tax Differentials and New Firm Location: Evidence from Panel Data." *Journal of Public Economics* 45 (June): 47–68.

Pechman, Joseph A. 1987. *Federal Tax Policy,* 5th ed. Brookings.

Pita, Claudino. 1993. "Exchange of Information between the Tax Administrations." Paper prepared for CIAT Technical Conference, Venice, Italy, November 1–5.

Plasschaert, Sylvain, ed. 1993. *Transnational Corporations: Transfer Pricing and Taxation.* Vol. 14 of the United Nations Library on Transnational Corporations. New York: United Nations.

Rädler, Alber J. 1993. "Where Does Tax Harmonization Stand Today?" *EC Tax Review* no. 4:198–99.

Razin, Assaf, and Efraim Sadka. 1991. "Vanishing Tax on Capital Income in the Open Economy." Working Paper 3796. Washington: National Bureau of Economic Research (August).

Schjelderup, Guttorm. 1993. "Optimal Taxation, Capital Mobility and Tax Evasion." *Scandinavian Journal of Economics* 95 (3): 377–86.

Shoup, Carl S. 1954. "Taxation Aspects of International Economic Integration." In *Aspects financiers et fiscaux de l'integration economique internationale,* 89–118. The Hague: Van Stockum.

Siebert, Horst, ed. 1990. *Reforming Capital Income Taxation.* Tübingen: J.C.B. Mohr.

Simons, Henry C. 1938. *Personal Income Taxation: The Definition of Income as a Problem of Fiscal Policy.* University of Chicago Press.

————. 1950. *Federal Tax Reform.* University of Chicago Press.

Sinn, Hans-Werner. 1989. "The Policy of Tax-Cut-Cum-Base Broadening: Implications for International Capital Movements." In *Public Finance and Performance of Enterprises,* edited by Manfred Neumann and Karl W. Roskamp, 153–176. Wayne State University Press.

Slemrod, Joel. 1990a. "Tax Havens, Tax Bargains and Tax Addresses: The Effect of Taxation on the Spatial Allocation of Capital." In *Reforming Capital Income Taxation,* edited by Horst Siebert, 23–42. Tübingen: J.C.B. Mohr.

————. 1990b. "Tax Principles in an International Economy." In *World Tax Reform: Case Studies of Developed and Developing Countries,* edited by Michael J. Boskin and Charles E. McLure, Jr., 11–23. San Francisco: ICS Press.

Smith, Stephen. 1993. "'Subsidiarity' and the Coordination of Indirect Taxes in the European Community." *Oxford Review of Economic Policy* 9 (Spring): 67–94.

Sørensen, Peter Birch. 1994. "From the Global Income Tax to the Dual Income Tax: Recent Tax Reforms in the Nordic Countries." *International Tax and Public Finance* 1 (May): 57–79.

Tait, Alan A. 1988. *Value Added Tax: International Practice and Problems*. Washington: International Monetary Fund.

――――. 1993. "Tax Harmonization, Economic Integration, and Growth: Some Issues Surveyed." Washington: International Monetary Fund (September).

Tannenwald, Robert. 1991. "The U.S. Tax Reform Act of 1986 and State Tax Competitiveness." In *Competition Among States and Local Governments: Efficiency and Equity in American Federalism*, edited by Daphne A. Kenyon and John Kincaid, 177–204. Washington: Urban Institute Press.

Tanzi, Vito. 1976. "Inflation, Indexation and Interest Income Taxation." *Banca Nazionale del Lavoro Quarterly Review* 116 (March): 64–76.

――――. 1980. "Inflationary Expectations, Economic Activity, Taxes, and Interest Rates." *American Economic Review* 70 (March): 12–21.

――――, ed., 1984. *Taxation, Inflation, and Interest Rates*. Washington: International Monetary Fund.

――――. 1986. "Public Expenditure and Public Debt: An International and Historical Perspective." In *Public Expenditure: The Key Issues*, edited by John Bristow and Declan McDonagh, 6–37. Dublin: Institute of Public Administration.

――――. 1989. "International Coordination of Fiscal Policies: Current and Future Issues." In *Fiscal Policy, Economic Adjustment, and Financial Markets*, edited by Marlo Monti, 7–37. Washington: International Monetary Fund.

Tanzi, Vito, and A. Lans Bovenberg. 1990. "Is There a Need for Harmonizing Capital Income Taxes within EC Countries?" In *Reforming Capital Income Taxation*, edited by Horst Siebert, 171–97. Tübingen: J.C.B. Mohr.

Tanzi, Vito, and Isaias Coelho. 1991. "Barriers to Foreign Investment in the U.S. and Other Nations." *Annals of the American Academy of Political and Social Science* 516 (July): 154–168.

――――. 1993. "Restrictions to Foreign Investment: A New Form of Protectionism?" In *Protectionism and World Welfare*, edited by Dominick Salvatore, 200–18. Cambridge University Press.

Tanzi, Vito, and Mark Lutz. 1993. "Interest Rates and Government Debt: Are the Linkages Global Rather than National?" In *The Political Economy of Government Debt*, edited by Harrie A.A. Verbon and Frans A.A.M. Van Winden, 233–54. New York: North Holland.

Tax Foundation. 1993. *Facts and Figures on Government Finance*. Washington.

United Nations. 1993. *World Investment Report, 1993: Transnational Corporations and Integrated International Production*. New York.

Valenduc, Christian. 1994. "Tax Havens and Fiscal Degradation in the European Community." *EC Tax Review* no. 1: 20–25.

Wasylenko, M. 1991. "Empirical Evidence and Interregional Business Location Decisions and the Role of Fiscal Incentives in Economic Development." In *Industry Location and Public Policy*, edited by Henry W. Herzog and Alan M. Schlottmann, 13–30. University of Tennessee Press.

Index